What Others Say

If You Could See Yourself, You Wouldn't Be Yourself is insightful and inspiring. On top of that, it is practical! My dear friend and brother in Christ, Rev. Dr. Stephen Lomax uses scriptural evidence to guide the reader into living their best and most blessed life by God.

This book enables us as believers to view ourselves in other people eyes. The author encourages the reader to see themselves beyond their own personal view through the eyes of God. This is a must-read!

—Reverend Dr. James Blassingame
Pastor of the Mount Zion Missionary Baptist Church, Sumter, SC
President of the SCE & M Convention,
Assistant Secretary of the National Baptist Convention, USA, INC.

Dr. Lomax's exploration of self-inventory gives us a glimpse of ourselves using the Word of God as the mirror. This Christian journey takes us into uncharted waters. However, the Word of God provides an excellent road map to provide guidance and encouragement.

If You Could See Yourself, You Wouldn't Be Yourself is a great resource for whatever challenges you may face. Dr. Stephen Lomax and I have been friends for over thirty years, and he has served as a pastor for that length of time as well. Let Dr. Lomax and his fifth commentary provide you with the necessary resources to assist you with navigating the goals of self as you travel in kingdom living.

—Dr. Robert L. McGowens, Sr.
Pastor, Greater Galilee Baptist Church-Charlotte Campus.
Charlotte, NC and Winston Salem Campus, WS, NC
2nd Vice Moderator, United Missionary Baptist Association.

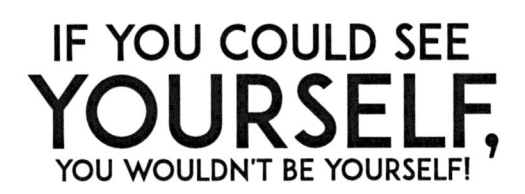

IF YOU COULD SEE YOURSELF,
YOU WOULDN'T BE YOURSELF!

IF YOU WANT TO BE YOUR BEST AND BE BLESSED BY GOD!

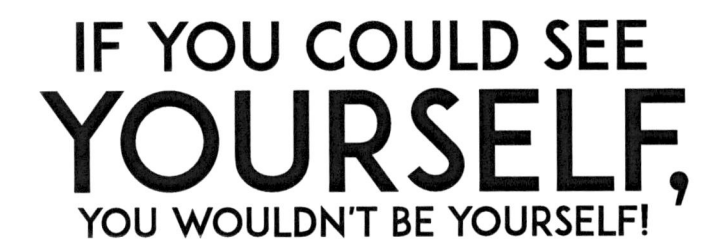

IF YOU COULD SEE YOURSELF,
YOU WOULDN'T BE YOURSELF!

STEPHEN LOMAX

TATE PUBLISHING
AND ENTERPRISES, LLC

If You Could See Yourself, You Wouldn't Be Yourself!
Copyright © 2016 by Stephen Lomax. All rights reserved.

No part of this publication may be reproduced, stored in a retrieval system or transmitted in any way by any means, electronic, mechanical, photocopy, recording or otherwise without the prior permission of the author except as provided by USA copyright law.

Scripture quotations marked (ESV) are from *The Holy Bible, English Standard Version*®, copyright © 2001 by Crossway Bibles, a publishing ministry of Good News Publishers. Used by permission. All rights reserved.

Scripture marked (GW) is taken from *GOD'S WORD*®. Copyright 1995 God's Word to the Nations. Used by permission of Baker Publishing Group. All rights reserved.

Scripture quotations marked (KJV) are taken from the *Holy Bible, King James Version, Cambridge*, 1769. Used by permission. All rights reserved.

Scripture quotations marked (MSG) are taken from *The Message*. Copyright © 1993, 1994, 1995, 1996, 2000, 2001, 2002. Used by permission of NavPress Publishing Group.

Scripture quotations marked (NIV) are taken from the *Holy Bible, New International Version*®, NIV®. Copyright © 1973, 1978, 1984 by Biblica, Inc.™ Used by permission of Zondervan. All rights reserved worldwide. www.zondervan.com

Scripture quotations marked (TLB) are taken from *The Living Bible* / Kenneth N. Taylor: Tyndale House, © Copyright 1997, 1971 by Tyndale House Publishers, Inc. Used by permission. All rights reserved.

The opinions expressed by the author are not necessarily those of Tate Publishing, LLC.

Published by Tate Publishing & Enterprises, LLC
127 E. Trade Center Terrace | Mustang, Oklahoma 73064 USA
1.888.361.9473 | www.tatepublishing.com

Tate Publishing is committed to excellence in the publishing industry. The company reflects the philosophy established by the founders, based on Psalm 68:11,
"The Lord gave the word and great was the company of those who published it."

Book design copyright © 2016 by Tate Publishing, LLC. All rights reserved.
Cover design by Norlan Balazo
Interior design by Gram Telen

Published in the United States of America

ISBN: 978-1-68352-864-7
Religion / Christian Life / Spiritual Growth
16.08.30

Acknowledgments

First, I must acknowledge God the Father, God the Son, and God the Holy Spirit for the inspiration, motivation, energy, courage, confidence, and knowledge to write the book. If it had not been for the Lord in my life, I don't know what I would do!

Second, I thank God for the love, support, and longevity of Mrs. Frances Delores Shaw Lomax. Your love and spiritual leadership has been superior down through the forty-three years of marriage.

May God richly bless you! If it had not been for you, I don't know what I would do. Thanks so much for all you do. From the depths of my heart and soul, I love you. Riding the roller coaster of life with you has been great, and I am still enjoying it. Thanks also for your contributions to the writing of this book. I'm looking forward to you writing your own book shortly.

To my children, Africa, Kenya, Stephanie, and Jerrell, I love you with agape (God's unlimited and nonexpectant) love. Over the years, you have brought your mother and me so much pride and joy that all of the money at Fort Knox could not buy. Love ya!

To my three sons-in-law (Todd, Jaron, and Greg), you have added much to the Lomax family, and I am proud to call you not only sons-in-law but sons. Keep up the good work, and may God bless you and your family. I am looking forward to Jerrell's wife becoming a part of the family soon.

To my grandchildren, Stephen Samuel Lomax II (Noot), Zhain Mckensie Roux (Ms. Roux), Zion Madison Roux, Frances Amani Mccomb. Ruby Sims (Ruby Red), Antonio Sims, and Erin Patterson. If I had only known what emotions of joy and fulfillment you would bring to my heart, I would have had you first.

I am waiting in great anticipation of another grandson's birth in August 2016. "To God be the glory for all of the wonderful things he hath done to the children of men." I cannot put into words, the deep love and happiness I feel just being in your presence. Stay close so that I can see you regularly and participate in your lives.

What can I say about the late Mrs. Ola Mae Henderson Lomax? Just a great, loving, wonderful, committed mother. Thanks so much for giving your all and all to your children, especially me, your youngest. Obviously, you will never be forgotten. Love you and miss you more than words can say.

To my dearly beloved brothers, the late Robert, James Willie (Quack), Noah, Luther, and my only remaining brother, Joe Louis. To my dearly beloved sisters, the late Dorothy and Thelma and my only remaining sister, Judy [husband James (Boot) Irby], thanks so much for the defense, love, and support over the years. It meant and still means so much to me. Also, thanks to your children, my nephew, James, and nieces, Jackie, Julie, Jatavia, for their support. Thanks also to my other nephews and niece in Philly and in SC, Noel, Bayshane, and Ola Louise.

To all the members of the New Life in Christ Missionary Baptist Church, mere words cannot describe the love, respect, and admiration I have for you. I am one of the few that have been greatly blessed with both of God's institutions—a great biological family and a great church family. Thank you so much for your commitment to righteousness in 2005 and continuance stance today.

You exemplify the words of the prophet Amos: "Let justice run down as waters and righteousness as a mighty stream" (Amos 5:24, kjv). I will never forget your dedication, devotion and support. "A family that prays together stays together." May heaven continue to smile upon you, your families, and the New Life in Christ Baptist Church as a whole; I know I will.

To Rev. Dr. James Blassingame, pastor of the Mount Zion Missionary Baptist Church, Sumter, SC, president of the SCE & M Convention, assistant secretary of the National Baptist Convention, USA, Inc, and my friend and seminary roommate for some of the classes at the Erskine Seminary. Thanks for your recommendation, confidence, and endorsement of my new book. May God continue to bless you and the family.

To another great pastor and friend down through the years, Rev. Dr. Robert Lee Mcgowens, senior pastor of the Greater Galilee Baptist Church, Charlotte, NC. Thanks for your kind and insightful words of endorsement. They are highly meaningful and reliable coming from both you and president Blassingame. May God continue to bless you, Terry, and the family.

To Sister Keah Kelressa Mitchell, New Life in Christ Church photographer. Thanks for all your time and effort to keep our ministry work out in the public eye. A special thanks for my photo on the rear cover of this book. A job well done. May God continue to bless and give you favor in photography and ministry.

Contents

Foreward 13
Foundation Scriptures! 15
Preface: God Wants You to Be Your Best 17
1 Introduction 21
2 Blind in One Eye and Can't See Out
   of the Other One! 27
3 Do the Devil's Work, Receive the Devil's Pay 35
4 If You Can't See, Turn on the Light! 45
5 Let This Mind Be in You 53
6 Man's Dilemma 65
7 Four Specific Steps to Seeing Yourself 77
8 A Friend in Need Is a Friend Indeed 101
9 Seeing What You Can't See 105
10 Open Eyes and Closed Minds 117
11 You Can Catch More Flies with Honey 131

Foreword

"**If You Could See Yourself, You Wouldn't Be Yourself**" is insightful and inspiring. On top of that, it is practical! My dear friend and brother in Christ, Rev. Dr. Stephen Lomax uses scriptural evidence to guide the reader into living their best and most blessed life by God.

This book enables us as believers to view ourselves in other people eyes. The author encourages the reader to see themselves beyond their own personal view through the eyes of God. **This is a must read**!

Reverend Dr. James Blassingame, pastor of the Mount Zion Missionary Baptist Church, Sumter, S. C. President of the S. C. E. & M Convention, Assistant Secretary of the National Baptist Convention, USA, INC.

Dr. Lomax's exploration of self-inventory, gives us a glimpse of ourselves using the Word of God as the mirror. This Christian journey takes us into uncharted waters. However the Word of God provides an excellent road map to provide guidance and encouragement.

"**If you could see yourself, you wouldn't be yourself**" is a great resource for whatever challenges you may face. Dr. Stephen Lomax and I have been friends for over 30 years and he has served as a pastor for that length of time as well. Let Dr. Lomax and his fifth commentary provide you with the necessary resources to assist you with navigating the goals of self as you travel in kingdom living.

Dr. Robert L. McGowens, Sr, Pastor- Greater Galilee Baptist Church- Charlotte Campus. Charlotte, NC. & Winston Salem Campus, WS, NC. 2nd Vice Moderator-United Missionary Baptist Association.

Foundation Scriptures!

Judge not, that ye be not judged. for what judgment ye judge, ye shall be judged: and with what measure ye mete, it shall be measured to you again. And why beholdest thou the mote that is in thy brother's eye, but considerest not the beam that is in thine own eye? Or how wilt thou say to thy brother, Let me pull out the mote out of thine eye; and, behold, a beam is in thine own eye? Thou hypocrite, first cast out the beam out of thine own eye; and then shalt thou see clearly to cast out the mote out of thy brother's eye. (Matt. 7:1–5)

Examine yourselves, to see whether you are in the faith. Test yourselves. Or do you not realize this about yourselves, that Jesus Christ is in you?—unless indeed you fail to meet the test!" (2 Cor. 13:5)

For if anyone is a hearer of the word and not a doer, he is like a man who looks intently at his natural face in a mirror. For he looks at himself and goes away and at once forgets what he was like. (James 1:23–24)

Do you see a man wise in his own eyes? There is more hope for a fool than for him. (Prov. 26:12)

Wolves in Sheep's Clothing!

Beware of false prophets, which come to you in sheep's clothing, but inwardly they are ravening wolves." (Matt. 7:15, KJV)

And just as they did not see fit to acknowledge God any longer, God gave them over to a depraved mind, to do those things which are not proper, being filled with all unrighteousness, wickedness, greed, evil; full of envy, murder, strife, deceit, malice; they are gossips, slanderers, haters of God, insolent, arrogant, boastful, inventors of evil, disobedient to parents, without understanding, untrustworthy, unloving, unmerciful; and, although they know the ordinance of God, that those who practice such things are worthy of death, they not only do the same, but also give hearty approval to those who practice them. (Rom. 1:28–32, NIV)

Now I urge you, brethren, keep your eye on those who cause dissensions and hindrances contrary to the teaching which you learned, and turn away from them. For such men are slaves, not of our Lord Christ but of their own appetites; and by their smooth and flattering speech they deceive the hearts of the unsuspecting. (Rom. 16:17–18, NIV)

Sheep in Sheep's Clothing! Be Real!

But the Lord said to Samuel, "Do not look on his appearance or on the height of his stature, because I have rejected him. For the Lord sees not as man sees: man looks on the outward appearance, but the Lord looks on the heart." (1 Sam. 16:7)

Do not let your adorning be external—the braiding of hair and the putting on of gold jewelry, or the clothing you wear—but let your adorning be the hidden person of the heart with the imperishable beauty of a gentle and quiet spirit, which in God's sight is very precious. (1 Pet. 3:3–4, KJV)

Preface

God Wants You to Be Your Best

The premise of the theme asserts that if people could see themselves as they really are, they would not be satisfied with themselves and therefore strive to become better, particularly if they want to become the person that they were created to be. Genesis 1:28 (LBT) says, "God blessed them and said, "Be fertile, increase in number, fill the earth, and be its master. Rule the fish in the sea, the birds in the sky, and all the animals that crawl on the earth." God's intent for man is to "be fruitful," be productive; and be actively working in order to be the best you can be. Please note that "as God worked six days and rested one" (the Sabbath), man needs to work six and rest one. Understand that to become your best, work six and rest one and associate with people of like work ethics. In other words, don't hang with, date, and, for heaven's sake, don't marry anyone who works one or two days and rests six or seven. I hope you understand what God is saying.

Further, to validate the premise of the book and make this effort of examination and hopefully a change in direction worthwhile, the first issue of necessity is affirming humanity becoming their best is commanded by God. The following study is a necessary step to this end. Please take the time to listen to God's voice as you meditate on his directives. "Blessed is the man that walketh not in the counsel of the ungodly, nor standeth in the way of sinners, nor sitteth in the seat of the scornful. But his delight is in the law of the Lord; and in his law doth he 'meditate' day and night."

Top of Form

> Whatever you do, work heartily, as for the Lord and not for men, knowing that from the Lord you will receive the inheritance as your reward. You are serving the Lord Christ. In other words, Work hard and cheerfully at all you do, just as though you were working for the Lord and not merely for your masters. (Col. 3:23–24)

2 Timothy 2:15 (TLB)

> Do your best to present yourself to God as one approved, a worker who has no need to be ashamed, rightly handling the word of truth. (2 Tim. 2:15)

TLB says, "Work hard so God can say to you, 'Well done.' Be a good workman, one who does not need to be ashamed when God examines your work. Know what his Word says and means."

> Do you not know that in a race all the runners run, but only one receives the prize? So run that you may obtain it. Every athlete exercises self-control in all things. They do it to receive a perishable wreath, but we an imperishable one. (1 Cor. 9:24–24, KJV)

TLB (The Living Bible) says, "In a race everyone runs, but only one person gets first prize. So run your race to win. To win the contest you must deny yourselves many things that would keep you from doing your best. An athlete goes to all this trouble just to win a blue ribbon or a silver cup, but we do it for a heavenly reward that never disappears."

> And whatever you do, in word or deed, do everything in the name of the Lord Jesus, giving thanks to God the Father through him. (Col. 3:17)

Give God the praise and always be thankful.

> The soul of the sluggard craves and gets nothing, while the soul of the diligent is richly supplied. (Prov. 13:4)

TLB says, "Lazy people want much but get little, while the diligent are prospering." The lazy have desires and wants, but they go unfulfilled, while the hard worker is blessed. Somebody said, "It's amazing how lucky the hard worker is."

> So, whether you eat or drink, or whatever you do, do all to the glory of God. (1 Cor. 10:31)
>
> A slack hand causes poverty, but the hand of the diligent makes rich. He who gathers in summer is a prudent son, but he who sleeps in harvest is a son who brings shame. (Prov. 10:4–5, KJV)
>
> Sloth makes you poor; diligence brings wealth. Make hay while the sun shines—that's smart; go fishing during harvest—that's stupid" (Prov. 10:4–5, MSG)
>
> Show yourself in all respects to be a model of good works, and in your teaching show integrity, dignity. And here you yourself must be an example to them of good deeds of every kind. Let everything you do reflect your love of the truth and the fact that you are in dead earnest about it. (Titus 2:7, ESV)
>
> Whatever your hand finds to do, do it with your might, for there is no work or thought or knowledge or wisdom in Sheol, to which you are going. (Eccles. 9:10)
>
> Remind them to be submissive to rulers and authorities, to be obedient, to be ready for every good work, to speak evil of no one, to avoid quarreling, to be gentle, and to show perfect courtesy toward all people. (Titus 3:1–2)
>
> But let each one test his own work, and then his reason to boast will be in himself alone and not in his neighbor. (Gal. 6:4)
>
> I can do all things through Christ who strengthens me. (Phil. 4:13)
>
> He will render to each one according to his works. (Rom. 2:6)
>
> Not everyone who says to me, "Lord, Lord," will enter the kingdom of heaven, but the one who does the will of my Father who is in heaven. On that day many will say to me, "Lord, Lord, did we not prophesy in your name, and cast out demons in your name, and do many mighty works in your name?" And then will I declare to them, "I never knew you; depart from me, you workers of lawlessness." (Matt. 7:21–23)

Therefore, if anyone is in Christ, he is a new creation. The old has passed away; behold, the new has come. (2 Cor. 5:17)

One who is taught the word must share all good things with the one who teaches. Do not be deceived: God is not mocked, for whatever one sows, that will he also reap. For the one who sows to his own flesh will from the flesh reap corruption, but the one who sows to the Spirit will from the Spirit reap eternal life. (Gal. 6:6–8)

Strive for peace with everyone, and for the holiness without which no one will see the Lord. (Heb. 12:14)

If the iron is blunt, and one does not sharpen the edge, he must use more strength, but wisdom helps one to succeed. (Eccles. 10:10)

Who serves as a soldier at his own expense? Who plants a vineyard without eating any of its fruit? Or who tends a flock without getting some of the milk? (1 Cor. 9:7)

Whoever speaks, as one who speaks oracles of God; whoever serves, as one who serves by the strength that God supplies—in order that in everything God may be glorified through Jesus Christ. To him belong glory and dominion forever and ever. Amen. (1 Pet. 4:11)

But as for the cowardly, the faithless, the detestable, as for murderers, the sexually immoral, sorcerers, idolaters, and all liars, their portion will be in the lake that burns with fire and sulfur, which is the second death. (Rev. 21:8)

Not neglecting to meet together, as is the habit of some, but encouraging one another, and all the more as you see the Day drawing near. (Heb. 10:25)

For if the readiness is there, it is acceptable according to what a person has, not according to what he does not have. (2 Cor. 8:12)

From the fruit of his mouth a man is satisfied with good, and the work of a man's hand comes back to him. (Prov. 12:14)

Go to the ant, O sluggard; consider her ways, and be wise. Without having any chief, officer, or ruler. (Prov. 6:6–7)

After reinforcing your biblical foundation with the above information, hopefully, now you are ready to build and begin your reformation! As Bishop T. D. Jakes says, "Get ready, get ready, get ready!"

1

Introduction

He is selfish, insecure, and negative! She is moody and manipulative! He is loud, rude, and talks too much about nothing! She is mean, hateful, and easily flies off of the handle! He is arrogant! She is a shady lady, both sexually and socially! He flirts with anything wearing a dress. She loves money and is too materialistic. He is violent and has fits of rage. She gossips seriously with strife, but when called on it, she says, she's just teasing and having fun. He drinks heavily on a regular basis, but he denies he has an alcohol problem. She has to have drugs to function and will smile in your face and stab you behind your back. He's a compulsive liar and tells one every other minute!

Neither of them holds truth high. They give their word, knowing they are not going to keep it. Neither can be trusted with people's personal information. They are like bad refrigerators: they can't keep anything. Carnal-mindedness (driven by fleshly impulses) leads them to pride, controlling, wishy-washy and never to the place of thanksgiving, no matter what is done for them. They think the world owes them something, and they walk around with a chip on their shoulder.

The imperative question that first needs addressing is whether or not you (the reader) is serious about becoming a better human being and being blessed by God. I dare you to be honest and answer this question: Do you see any resemblance of yourself to the man or woman just described above? Concentrate solely on yourself for a moment. Dismiss the distraction to focus on others and their characteristics. For instance, your husband, wife, friend, coworker, or fellow church member might be mean or nasty, but resist the temptation to focus on them; look instead only at yourself. This is a personal exercise for your growth. Are you mean, nasty, and without much patience?

This book was written to help you become better and be blessed by God. (Though, it would be great, if the key people in your life would read it as well. Then all of the adjusting and correction will not be on you alone. I recommend giving a copy of this book to your significant other, children, close friends, work companions, and loved ones.) But for now, you personally should consider the question of the theme: "If you could see yourself, flaws and all, would you be yourself?"

Hopefully you said no and would not remain selfish, disobedient, and rebellious. Hopefully you would not want to be a wolf in sheep's clothing but become a sheep in sheep's clothing. In other words, just be real, especially considering what is at stake. What is at stake, whether or not you become the best you can be and be blessed by God or cursed? It has been proven to you already in the Scripture exercise above that God commands you to become your best. Exercise your faith, for without faith, it is impossible to please God. Hebrews 11:6 reminds all, "But without faith it is impossible to please him: for he that cometh to God must believe that he is, and that he is a rewarder of them that diligently seek him." What I am saying is this, get real, get better, and get blessed by God. Learn the lesson of King Saul.

Saul slipped into the deadly snare of many religious people. He did not mind offering sacrifices to God, but afterward, he would slip back into following the impulses of his heart. Saul tried to use religion as a smokescreen to cover the ungodliness of his life. It will never work. God sees right through it! Some people say, "I go to church! I take communion! I went to a bible conference and revival last year and heard some of the best Christian speakers around!" It doesn't matter if it does not do you any good and you continue to walk in disobedience! Rebellion, presumption, and disobedience were three strikes against Saul. Then Saul heard words from Samuel that were as awful for Samuel to speak as they were for Saul to hear: "Because you have rejected the word of the Lord, he has also rejected you from being king" (1 Sam. 15:23).

Let me further prove my point. 1 Peter 3:9 (NLT) says, "Don't repay evil for evil. Don't retaliate with insults when people insult you. Instead, pay them back with a blessing. That is what God has called you to do, and he will bless you for it." In Matthew 5:11, Jesus said, "Blessed are you when people insult you, persecute you and falsely say all kinds of evil against you because of me. Rejoice and be glad, because great is your reward in heaven, for in the same way they persecuted the prophets who were before you."

Remember the Golden Rule: "Do unto others as you would have them to do you" (Luke 6:31) and be blessed by God for your effort. Also, remember the silver rule: "Don't do to others what you don't want done to you."

Psalm 119:2 says, "Blessed are those who keep his statutes and seek him with all their heart." You will be happier and more content when you do things God's way. His way is the best way for humanity because as the Creator (manufacturer), God knows what we need and what's best for us better than anyone.

Psalm 24:1–5 says,

> The earth is the LORD's, and the fullness thereof; the world, and they that dwell therein. For he hath founded it upon the seas, and established it upon the floods. Who shall ascend into the hill of the LORD? or who shall stand in his holy place? He that hath clean hands, and a pure heart; who hath not lifted up his soul unto vanity, nor sworn deceitfully. He shall receive the blessing from the LORD, and righteousness from the God of his salvation.

Acknowledge God as the Creator, Owner, and Sustainer of all human kind. Then live like it and God will bless you.

Psalm 1:1 says,

> Blessed is the man that walketh not in the counsel of the ungodly, nor standeth in the way of sinners, nor sitteth in the seat of the scornful. But his delight is in the law of the Lord and in his law doth he meditate day and night. And he shall be like a tree planted by the rivers of water, that bringeth forth his fruit in his season; his leaf also shall not wither; and whatsoever he doeth shall prosper. The ungodly are not so: but are like the chaff which the wind driveth away. Therefore the ungodly shall not stand in the judgment, nor sinners in the congregation of the righteous. For the Lord knoweth the way of the righteous: but the way of the ungodly shall perish.

What is David saying? He's saying that you should choose your friends and acquaintances carefully. In fact, meditate and pray before making decision on relationships, whether personal or business. The person that does these things in the Lord will receive nourishment like a tree planted by the rivers of water. But for those that disobey God's words, life will be unstable as the leaves blowing in the wind.

Proverbs 16:18–20, says, "Pride goes before destruction, a haughty spirit before a fall." It is better to be humble in spirit with the lowly peasant, than todivide the spoil with the proud. He who gives attention to the word will find good; and be blessed because he trusts in the LORD." In the simplest terms, the verse reworded says, "The love of yourself builds a path to your destruction, and a prideful, arrogant air or spirit will cause hurt and pain." When pride rules your lives, your love, depend and care only for yourselves and what you want.

Take note that the evil characteristic of pride led to Satan's expulsion from heaven (Ezek. 28:17 and Isa. 14). Once again, meditate on the characterizations made about the man and woman above. I believe you will agree that there are millions of people walking the face of the earth just like them—selfish, hateful, rude, mean, manipulative, arrogant, controlling, sexually immoral, impure, sensual, idol worshippers, have enmity (full of animosity), jealous, angry, rivals, dissentful, divided, envious, heavy drinkers (or drunks), drug addicts, lovers of porn, orgies, open marriages, and things like these" (1 Cor. 6:8–9, NIV).

Yet it's hard pressed to find people acknowledging their membership among any of these groups. One of the best examples seen today is this: people participating in so-called "open marriages," even wanting their "open marriages" to be kept closed and secretively hidden. Isn't that ironic? It shines the spotlight of man's depravity on his refusal to acknowledge his negative activity. It's simply amazing, given the great numbers of people involved, to find so few people willing to admit their weakness.

In words, there may possibly be a few people that acknowledge their imperfection. They say, "Nobody's perfect," acknowledging the threshold of perfection is a hard line to uphold. Yet they add quickly, "Nobody's perfect but Jesus Christ; and he was the Son of the Living God." But notice this, even when a human being acknowledges his/her imperfection, when asked to describe the fault, these same human beings are reluctant to discuss any. Why is this? you ask. And why can't people see their own faults and fallacies? This is a great question and one the book sets out to answer.

If you are still wondering, why the effort, the effort is well worth the energy spent because the possibilities of human enrichment are unlimited. Think about it for just a minute. If somehow man is able to overcome this gigantic weakness of human accountability, what a different world this would become! If humans could see themselves as they really are and how they are seen by others, it would revolutionize the world.

Though a great challenge, it is one that can be met. Are you willing to search within yourself to see yourself as you really are and investigate your view by others? It is a major challenge, but it is necessary to point mankind in the right direction of achieving a higher state of civilization.

2

Blind in One Eye and Can't See Out of the Other One!

It is imperative to closely examine the reasons why so many people are adamant about their names *not* being included on the list of people with issues. The first reason could be simply that they just don't see themselves accurately and really don't see any connection to the negative attributes the Bible lists. Maybe there are many people who are not playing games or plotting any schemes to fool anyone, and they just don't see themselves as possessing negativity.

It could be just that simple. As the older folk used to say, "They are blind in one eye and can't see out of the other one." Whether this is true or not, in order to eliminate the debate and "the reaping what you sow" reality for possessing this blind truth (if indeed it is blindness), the first step necessary is to pause, examine, and define negativity. Negativity is the expression of criticism of or pessimism about something. This defining is necessary for both accuracy and assurance so that no person reading this book will fail to become their best due to blind ignorance or devilish misunderstanding.

First here's the definition of the attribute "selfishness."

Caution: in order to gain the most assistance from this book, while reading this chapter, stop and reflect on yourself. This requires genuine and honest self-reflection. Resist the temptation to point fingers at others.

Remember the man and woman from chapter 1 who were said to be selfish. (Note: All of the following definitions are given by Wikipedia, the free encyclopedia, unless otherwise indicated.) Selfishness or selfish people are concerned sometimes excessively or exclusively, for oneself or one's own advantage, pleasure, or welfare; regardless of others. *Selfishness* is the opposite of altruism or selflessness. All selfish people display a very uncaring attitude and a strong "me first" trait.

Selfishness is a very peculiar and common trait that "all" selfish and conceited people possess (Wikipedia). They always put themselves and their needs at the front of the line. They only give heed to others when it serves their interests, priorities and goals. They seldom think of other's interest or needs, not even those who might be less fortunate than them.

Selfish people have tendencies to make statements beginning with "I, my, and me." Examples: "This is my house, my money, my clothes, my car, my children and grandchildren and my time," etc. "I own this, I bought this and I will do with it as I please." On the other hand, quickly notice the opposite. Jesus's use of the word "my" was ownership but not materialistic." Jesus's use was spiritual. He said, "Upon this rock, I will build my church." He said, "My disciples," "my father which art in heaven, etc." Be aware of how you use "I, me, and my."

Another trait that selfish and conceited people demonstrate is manipulation (scheming and plotting to get one's way). This trait arises from the fact that selfish people are driven by fear of loss (possessions, position, control, etc.). To them possessions, position, control, etc. represent power, and power validates their self-worth. They think, "If I don't possess power and exercise it, I am nobody." Or at least, this is how they feel they are viewed by the world. Therefore, they must do whatever it takes—or as some have said, "by any means necessary" to attain power, possessions, and position.

Also, they are calculative and accumulators. Oscar Wilde, the Irish writer-poet, expressed this trait this way, "There are many things that selfish people would throw away if they were not afraid that others might pick them up." Thereby, selfish people tend to hold on to things and hoard them to themselves, and sometimes this includes hoarding people. Many times, selfish parents try to hold on to their children.

This is done in a variety of ways. One way is when they try to keep them from living their own lives. The evidence of this is revealed when they try to relive their lives through their children. For instance, they try to force their children to participate in pageants, sports, etc. because they always wanted to be a beauty queen or athlete. This is the parent's dream, not their children's. Parents must be mindful and considerate of their children. Remember that you have lived your lives; let them live theirs.

Selfish people have low self-esteem. Low self-esteem gives them a negative outlook toward life and generally makes them contemptuous of others. It makes them scornful, disdainful, disrespectful, and insultingly sneering. This negative trait toward everything and everybody makes them bad team players. With their actions, suggestions, and remarks, they try to tear down, never to build up.

Here's another identifying trait. In the basketball game of life, they always want the ball in their hands. It's not because the game is on the line and they have more talent to score or get the job done; selfish people just don't like passing the ball of power, position, or possession. They want all eyes on them. Reader, think about yourself. Do you consistently seek attention and crave for the ball of decision and control in your hands? Be honest and be helped! Remember the warning of this chapter. In order to be helped, you must be honest and look within! God warns before taking action. Hebrews 11:7 says, "By faith Noah, being warned of God of things not seen as yet, moved with fear, prepared an ark to the saving of his house; by the which he condemned the world, and became heir of the righteousness which is by faith."

Heed the warning and strive to know yourself. How can you expect others to know you and please you when you don't know yourself? How can you expect people around you to give you what you want, when you don't know yourself what you want? In such a state of self-ignorance, a person cannot be happy, and the people around you cannot be either. You get upset for receiving apples, but you asked for apples. If you don't know you don't like apples, how in the world is anyone else going to know it? Know yourself and fix yourself!

Selfish people find it hard to motivate and inspire others. They lack motivation and the drive for success on a high level. This characteristic makes them unpopular in the team concept and an outsider at group tasks. Even their love relationships are dysfunctional, and in society, they are uncomfortable as well.

Selfish people are highly self-centered and self-obsessed. This trait makes it harder for them to see or hear other people's concerns. Jeremiah 5:21 describes this reality. God says, "Hear now this, O foolish people, and without understanding; which have eyes, and see not; which have ears, and hear not." In Mark 18:8, Jesus said, "Having eyes, see ye not, and having ears, hear ye not? And do ye not remember?"

Not hearing and seeing other's concerns, selfish people become bad listeners. They give little or no consideration to what others say and do. They are inconsiderate, which demonstrates little or no compassion. They rudely cut off the conversations of others to bring the focus back on themselves. Their desire to be seen and heard more than anyone else makes them oblivious to the opinions, suggestions, and advice of others. The conversations they indulge in pertain somehow to themselves.

If these characteristics remind you of anybody, particularly if it's you, I hope you will acknowledge, admit it, and then take steps to change. James 3:16–17 says, "For where jealousy and selfish ambition exist, there will be disorder and every vile practice. But the wisdom from above is first pure, then peaceable, gentle, open to reason, full of mercy and good fruits, impartial and sincere." Dr. Martin Luther King Jr. said, "Nothing in all the world is more dangerous than sincere ignorance and conscientious stupidity."

Additionally, an unknown poet said, "Selfish people lose so much in life because even when they realize they are wrong, they don't know how to correct it. They don't even know how to ask for forgiveness or show regret." In Matthew 18:15, Jesus's gave directives on the subject. He said, "Moreover if thy brother shall trespass against thee, go and tell him his fault between thee and him alone: if he shall hear thee, thou hast gained thy brother." Remember, "He who is full of God, can never be full of Himself." Jesus said, "No man can serve two Masters, for he will hate the one and love the other" (Matt. 6:24).

The second negative attribute needing investigation is *meanness*, or *hatred*. Meanness is defined as lacking in kindness; unkind, cruel, spiteful, and malicious; expressing spite or malice; tending toward or characterized by cruelty or violence; extremely unpleasant or disagreeable.

1. Mean people use hurtful words. Mean people have learned the gift of complimentary insults. They have trouble complimenting. Instead, they say, "This dinner was amazing. Who made it? I know it wasn't you!" They say, "Girl, that dress is fitting you, but you would look even greater if you lost a few pounds." Somehow, they know

how to string words together, in order to inflict the maximum amount of hurt and pain even while trying to put it nicely.

2. Mean people play the blame game. When dealing with mean people, it becomes obvious quickly that they blame everyone but themselves for any and everything. I read an article where a person was speeding through a red light in a school zone, ran over an old lady in a wheelchair, and tried to place the blame on granny. Do you take responsibility for your actions or look to blame the "grannies" in your life?

3. Hatred: According to the Open Criminology Journal of 2013, in an article entitled "The Psychology of Hatred," "Hatred is a strong, negative feeling against the object of the hatred. The hater sees the object of their hatred as bad, immoral, dangerous, or all of this together (Staub, 2003). Violent acts are also acts of hatred, when based on an intense, persistent and negative perception of the other. Especially when the intent and desire is to hurt, destroy, or even make suffer. Hatred is based on the perception of the other. But also has a strong relationship with people personally, their own personal history, and effects their personality, feelings, ideas, beliefs, and especially, identity. Certain adversity in life triggers and intensifies hatred: jealousy, failure, guilt and so on."

4. Arrogance. Further to help men and women better see themselves, the fourth most common attribute of examination is *arrogance*. Arrogance is an insulting way of thinking or behaving that comes from believing that you are better, smarter, or more important than other people.

Ways to determine if you are arrogant

- You offend many people! Arrogant people seem to have a knack for offending others. Do you find that you offend people much and think it's always there fault?
- You believe you always know better than other people! New Life in Christ Baptist Church slogan is "The Church where everybody is somebody and nobody but Christ knows it all." Understand that no one knows everything but Christ,

no matter what education or standing one may have in the church or world.

- You are constantly late! It could be a signal that you just have a problem with being punctual or that you underestimate how long it takes you to get ready, if not done on a regular basis. But on regular basis, it signals that you feel your time is more valuable than others and that people should wait on you.

- You have a habit of interrupting people. Sometimes people interrupt others a lot because it is a bad habit. Sometimes they just do it unintentionally and without thought. But arrogant people interrupt because they think and feel that what they have to say is more important than what someone else is saying. They think their statement has such importance that it gives them the right to talk over someone.

- Lastly, you believe you are better than others. Arrogant people not only think that they know better than others but believe they are better. They see themselves as above others in looks, intelligence, actions, finances, or many other ways. It is wonderful to have good self-esteem, to know your talent and to be proud of them, but if you think you are better than others in any way, stop, take a good look at yourself, and consider what God says: "For if a man think himself to be something, when he is nothing, he deceiveth himself" (Gal. 6:3, KJV).

Obviously, from the list of negative attributes, there are many others that could be broken down and examined, but here is the fifth and final one the book will address.

5. Drug addiction. The Bible warns against drug addiction: Proverbs 20:1 says, "Wine is a mocker, strong drink a brawler, and whoever is led astray by it is not wise. "1 Corinthians 6:9–11 says, "Or do you not know that the unrighteous will not inherit the kingdom of God? Do not be deceived: neither the sexually immoral, nor idolaters, nor adulterers, nor men (people) who practice homosexuality, nor thieves, nor the greedy, nor drunkards, nor revilers, nor swindlers will inherit the kingdom of God. And such were some of you. But you were washed, sanctified, and justified in

the name of the Lord Jesus Christ and by the Spirit of our God." Ephesians 5:18 says, "And do not get drunk with wine, for that is debauchery (indulgence in sensual pleasures; scandalous activities involving sex, alcohol, or drugs without inhibition), but be filled with the Spirit."

Additionally, note the following information taken from the National Council on Alcohol and Drug Dependency.

To assist you in identifying your condition, the following symptoms associated with alcohol abuse are outlined:

1. Temporary blackouts or memory loss.
2. Recurrent arguments or fights with family members or friends as well as irritability, depression, or mood swings.
3. Continuing use of alcohol to relax, to cheer up, to sleep, to deal with problems, or to feel "normal."
4. Headache, anxiety, insomnia, nausea, or other unpleasant symptoms when one stops drinking. Flushed skin and broken capillaries on the face; a husky voice; trembling hands; bloody or black/tarry stools or vomiting blood; chronic diarrhoea.
5. Drinking alone, in the mornings, or in secret.

Signs in general of addiction:

1. Loss of Control: Drinking or drugging more than a person wants to, for longer than they intended (despite telling themselves that they wouldn't do it).
2. Neglecting Activities: Spending less time on activities that used to be important (hanging out with family and friends, exercising, pursuing hobbies or other interests). Due to the use of alcohol or drugs; there has been a drop in attendance and performance at work or school.
3. Risk Taking: More likely to take serious risks in order to obtain one's drug of choice.
4. Relationship Issues: People struggling with addiction are known to act out against those closest to them, particularly if someone is

attempting to address their substance problems; complaints from co-workers, supervisors, teachers or classmates.

5. Secrecy: Going out of one's way to hide the amount of drugs or alcohol consumed or one's activities when drinking or drugging; unexplained injuries or accidents.

6. Changing appearance: Serious changes or deterioration in hygiene or physical appearance—lack of showering, slovenly (messy and dirty) appearance, unclean clothes.

7. Family History: A family history of addiction can dramatically increase one's predisposition to substance abuse.

8. Tolerance: Over time, a person's body adapts to a substance to the point that they need more and more of it in order to have the same reaction.

9. Withdrawal: As the effect of the alcohol or drugs wears off, the person may experience symptoms such as: anxiety or jumpiness; shakiness or trembling; sweating, nausea and vomiting, insomnia, depression, irritability, fatigue or loss of appetite and headaches.

10. Continued Use Despite Negative Consequences: Even though it is causing problems (on the job, in relationships, for one's health), a person continues drinking and drugging.

Do you know of anyone with these symptoms? Again, if it's you, acknowledge it and seek and accept assistance! In the long run, you will not regret it.

3

Do the Devil's Work, Receive the Devil's Pay

If you are not a theologian or a serious Bible reader, you probably missed the biblical foundation of the book's theme. The previous list of fleshly desires and negative attributes are straight from the Word of God. Specifically, they were directly taken from the epistle of Galatians 5:19–21, where Paul characterizes them as "the works of the flesh," particularly Galatians 5:16–18, where Paul encourages Christians to live by the Spirit of God and not gratify the desires of the sinful nature. Additionally, Luke 9:23 (NLT) says, "Then he said to the crowd, If any of you wants to be my follower, you must turn from your selfish ways, take up your cross daily, and follow me."

Galatians 5:17 records Paul's words: "For the sinful nature desires what is contrary to the Spirit, and the Spirit what is contrary to the sinful nature. They are in conflict with each other, so that you do not do what you want. But if you are led by the Spirit, you are not under law." The law was given for direction, but if you are led by the Spirit, you already have the direction of God through the Spirit.

Before Christ, the natural's man's heart is corrupt (total depravity)!

Jeremiah put it this way: "The heart is deceitful above all things and beyond cure. Who can understand it" (Jer. 17:9).

The Scripture teaching is that man in his present fallen state is basically evil. He is deceitful and conniving. Yes, there is good in him because of his formation and the remnant of God's image is still present. But the good has been corrupted. No part of man is any longer perfectly good as he was created. Genesis 1:31 says, "And God saw everything that he had made, and, behold, *it was* very good." But since the "Fall," mankind is a mixture of good and evil. And certainly man's "flesh" is corrupt: Paul said,

"For I know that good itself does not dwell in me, that is, in my sinful nature (flesh). For I have the desire to do what is good, but I cannot carry it out" (Rom. 7:18).

All is somewhat corrupt, and therefore, even the "good" in man cannot be trusted. Jesus revealed this when he taught on the heart or core of man: He said, "The things that come out of the mouth come from the heart, and these make a man 'unclean.' For out of the heart come evil thoughts, murder, adultery, sexual immorality, theft, false testimony, slander. These are what make a man 'unclean'" (Matt. 15:18–20a).

Again, Paul's teaching is about the flesh. Theologians have since framed this condition as the doctrine of total depravity. Not that man has absolutely no good in him. But that in every aspect man is flawed. Even the good that a person intends come from mixed motives, such as personal preference, gain, and selfishness, thus revealing the need to both know and see oneself.

In Galatians 5:19, Paul specifically lists the works that gratify the desires of the sinful flesh. In reality, it is not a curse as many people perceive it to be. But in fact, it is a great blessing to mankind because in it, God removes all doubt, discussion, and debate. There is no guesswork as to how God feels about these acts.

The conclusion is obvious: people in their right minds (defined as those concerned about their spiritual well-being and connection to God) don't want to be identified as sinful followers of the flesh and opposing the will of God. 1 Peter 2:11 says, "Dearly beloved, I beseech you as strangers and pilgrims, abstain from fleshly lusts, which war against the soul."

The Prodigal Son

Note Luke 15:13–17. Jesus spoke of man known as the prodigal son

> Not long after the conversation with his father, the younger son got together all he had, set off for a distant country and there squandered his wealth in wild living. After he had spent everything, there was a severe famine in that whole country, and he began to be in need. So he went and hired himself out to a citizen of that country, who sent him to his fields to feed pigs. He longed to fill his stomach with the pods that the pigs were eating, but no one gave him anything.
>
> When he came to his senses, he said, "How many of my father's hired servants have food to spare, and here I am starving to death! I

will set out and go back to my father and say to him: Father, I have sinned against heaven and against you."

Sin is a designation of God, and he alone determines what sin is and how to be forgiven for it. The prodigal son acknowledges sin as such in the story Christ discussed.

As previously seen, following the desires of the flesh is dangerous both physically and spiritually. How many people (and maybe at some point, you were one of them) have found themselves in trouble following the desires of the flesh? How many relationships have been destroyed by one or both partners following their fleshly desire to commit adultery? How many relationships have been destroyed by people lying to each other and stealing from one another or stealing from some other third party?

How many relationships have been broken by people, sick and tired of dealing with mean, selfish, ungrateful, and negative people? How many relationships have been destroyed by verbal and physical abuse? What about drunkenness, drugs, and alcohol? How many people have you heard say, "I just couldn't take it anymore?"

Need I remind you that these are the works of the flesh as inspired by the prince of this world, the devil? Ephesians 2:1–3 says, "And you were dead in your trespasses and sins, in which you formerly walked according to the course of this world, according to the prince of the power of the air, of the spirit that is now working in the sons of disobedience. Among them we too all formerly lived in the lusts of our flesh, indulging the desires of the flesh and of the mind, and were by nature children of wrath, even as the rest.

Cleary, it's self-destructive and dangerous to follow the flesh. Can you say it out loud? It's self-destructive and dangerous to follow the flesh. The psychologists and theologian say, there's something about speaking words. Words have power. The world was created by God speaking words. Psalm 33:9 says, "For he spake and it was done; he commanded, and it stood fast." Hebrews 11:3 says, "By faith we understand that the universe was formed at God's command, so that what is seen was not made out of what was visible." Proverbs 18:21(NKJV) says, "Death and life are in the power of the tongue: and they that love it shall eat the fruit thereof."

There's power in the spoken language and saying the right words. So say it again out loud: "It's self-destructive and dangerous to follow the flesh." Additionally, saying it means you have both acknowledged and absorbed it. Speaking something helps you get it into your intellectual spirit. Once again, "It's self-destructive and dangerous to follow the flesh." Yes it is. Romans 8:7 (NLB) says this: "For the sinful nature is always hostile to God. It never did obey God's laws, and it never will." Let's be absolutely clear: if people are not following God, who are they following? Paul says they are following their sinful nature, which is manifested in their fleshly desires.

Additionally, concerning men and women's fleshly desires, which Paul declared is against God; there is the devil operating behind the scene. 1 Chronicles 21:1 reminds us, "And Satan stood up against Israel, and provoked David to number Israel." David was provoked, incited, and moved to act destructively by Satan, the devil. This means that David's idea, impulse, and direction to move to action on his destructive thoughts came from Satan. Satan incited David to take the census, knowing that God would be displeased. Satan is destructive and rebellious. His acts are always negative, hurtful, and harmful. The following Scripture details his devices and devastation: In 2 Corinthians 2:11, it says, "Lest Satan should get an advantage of us: for we are not ignorant of his devices.

Satan is known to accuse the brethren. Revelation 12:10 says, "Then I heard a loud voice in heaven say: "Now have come the salvation and the power and the kingdom of our God, and the authority of his Messiah. For the accuser (Satan) of our brothers and sisters, who accuses them before our God day and night, has been hurled down."

He tempts the Christian. In 1 Corinthians 7:5, it says, "Do not deprive each other except perhaps by mutual consent and for a time, so that you may devote yourselves to prayer. Then come together again so that Satan will not tempt you because of your lack of self-control."

He tries to take the Christian captive at his will. In 2 Timothy 2:26, it says, "And that they may recover themselves out of the snare of the devil, who are taken captive by him at his will."

He tries to hinder the Christian in his work for the Lord. In 1 Thessalonians 2:18, it says, "Wherefore we would have come unto you, even I Paul, once and again; but Satan hindered us." He buffets the Christian; force one's way by a fight, struggle: The verse of 2 Cor. 12:7 describes Satan's buffeting Paul.

He desires to sift the Christian as wheat; to break you down. Luke 22:31 says, "And the Lord said, Simon, Simon, behold, Satan hath desired to have you, that he may sift you as wheat."

He tries to get the Christian to blaspheme God. In 1 Timothy 1:20, Paul said, "Among them are Hymenaeus and Alexander, whom I have handed over to Satan to be taught not to blaspheme."

He tries to get an advantage of the Christian. In 2 Corinthians 2:11, it says, "Lest Satan should get an advantage of us: for we are not ignorant of his devices."

He tries to beguile the Christian; charm or enchant (someone), in a deceptive way. In 2 Corinthians 11:3, it says, "But I am afraid that just as Eve was deceived by the serpent's cunning, your minds may somehow be led astray from your sincere and pure devotion to Christ."

He blinds the minds of the nonbeliever. In 2 Corinthians 4:4, it says, "The god of this age has blinded the minds of unbelievers, so that they cannot see the light of the gospel that displays the glory of Christ, who is the image of God."

He seeks to devour the Christian. In 1 Peter 5:8, it says, "Be alert and of sober mind. Your enemy the devil prowls around like a roaring lion looking for someone to devour." In 2 Corinthians 11:3, it says, "But I am afraid that just as Eve was deceived by the serpent's cunning, your minds may somehow be led astray from your sincere and pure devotion to Christ."

In 1 Chronicles 21, the provoking of David by Satan cost seventy thousand Israelites to lose their lives. Moreover, Matthew 6:24 declares, "There are Two Spirits in control, God and mammon (Material things of the Devil). All people follow one or the other. Specifically Jesus said, "No man can serve two Masters, he will hate the one and love the other. You cannot serve God and mammon."

Take note that the sinful attributes of the flesh originated with Lucifer, the archangel (devil, Satan) who God threw out of heaven into the earth. In Matthew 10:17–20, note what Jesus says: "The seventy returned with joy, saying, 'Lord, even the demons are subject to us in your name.' And He said to them, 'I was watching Satan fall from heaven like lightning. Behold, I have given you authority to tread on serpents and scorpions, and over all the power of the enemy and nothing will injure you. Nevertheless do not rejoice in this, that the spirits are subject to you, but rejoice that your names are recorded in heaven.'"

Ezekiel 28:14–17 (NIV) gives further background. It says, "You were anointed as a guardian cherub, for so I ordained you. You were on the holy mount of God; you walked among the fiery stones. You were blameless in your ways from the day you were created till **wickedness** was found in you. Through your widespread trade you were filled with **violence**, and you sinned. So I drove you in disgrace from the mount of God, and I expelled you, guardian cherub, from among the fiery stones. Your heart became **proud** on account of **your beauty**, and you **corrupted** your wisdom because of your splendor. So I threw you to the earth."(For more information on the origin of the Satan, see Isaiah 14:13–14).

Notice the words in bold letters describing the attributes of Lucifer (Satan, devil): wickedness, violence, pride because of beauty, and corruption. Jesus describes Satan (Lucifer, devil):John 8:43–44 (RSV) says, "Why do you not understand what I say? It is because you cannot bear to hear my word. You are of your father the devil, and your will is to do your father's desires. He was a murderer from the beginning, and has nothing to do with the truth, because there is no truth in him. When he lies, he speaks according to his own nature, for he is a liar and the father of lies."

The similarities between the desires of human flesh and the attributes of the devil are too astounding to miss. Note that both have the same goals (to destroy) and the same fate (being destroyed). Matthew 25:41 (KJV) says, "Jesus said, then shall he say also unto them on the left hand, depart from me, ye cursed, into everlasting fire, prepared for the devil and his angels: For I was an hungred, and ye gave me no meat: I was thirsty, and ye gave me no drink: I was a stranger, and ye took me not in: naked, and ye clothed me not: sick, and in prison, and ye visited me not. Then shall they also answer him, saying, Lord, when saw we thee a hungred, or athirst, or a stranger, or naked, or sick, or in prison, and did not minister unto thee? Then shall he answer them, saying, verily I say unto you, Inasmuch as ye did it not to one of the least of these, ye did it not to me. And these shall go away into everlasting punishment: but the righteous into life eternal."

As you can see, the need for people to see themselves as they are goes far beyond just being blessed but really is a life-and-death matter.

Preachers, teachers, and leaders, listen up! Practice what you preach and do before you teach! Hebrews 11:7 says, "By faith Noah, being warned of God of things not seen as yet, moved with fear, prepared an ark to the saving of his house; by the which he condemned the world, and became heir of the righteousness which is by faith."

God could have built the ark, but he clearly commanded man to build it. God could have delivered the children of Israel without Moses, but he sent him to do it. God demands man's participation! "Faith without works is dead" (James 2:14).

Second, after finishing the discussion why man must not be ruled by negativity, allow me the privilege to share some personal self-examination declarations. Hopefully these will be a testimony to some people searching for satisfaction in the Christian life. The first declaration acknowledges Jesus's caution that every effective Christian action must begin with self-examination. I will follow this example myself. Note first his biblical cautions. In 2 Corinthians 13:5, it says, "Test yourselves to see if you are in the faith; examine yourselves! Or do you not recognize this about yourselves; that Jesus Christ is in you—unless indeed you fail the test?"

James 3:1 says, "Not many of you should become teachers, my brothers, for you know that we who teach will be judged with greater strictness." In other words, you had better practice what you preach. Acts 1:8 says, "But ye shall receive power, after that the Holy Ghost is come upon you: and ye shall be witnesses unto me both in Jerusalem (self, home, friends, etc.), and in all Judæa, and in Samaria, and unto the uttermost part of the earth." After you are saved, the Holy Ghost is available to you, and you shall witness for Jesus.

Revelation 2:1–2 says, "To the angel of the church in Ephesus write, the words of him who holds the seven stars in his right hand, who walks among the seven golden lampstands. I know your works, your toil and your patient endurance, and how you cannot bear with those who are evil, but have tested those who call themselves apostles and are not, and found them to be false."

In other words, John was saying, "I know you are enduring patiently and bearing up for my name's sake, and you have not grown weary. But I have this against you; that you have abandoned the love you had at first. Remember therefore from where you have fallen; repent, and do the works you did at first. If not, I will come to you and remove your lampstand from its place, unless you repent." Based on these exhortations, for me to be the kind of person I need to be and God wants me to be, I need to see myself for myself. I need to get my own house in order. But it is important to take note of how others see me so I can be an effective witness to others with power and integrity.

Please notice that I did not say that I would be a witness only, but I said I must be an effective witness, having power and integrity. This kind of witnessing comes only by practicing what you preach and learning to do before you teach. Personally, I would not act on a person's witness to me on how to get a new car, if he/she is driving a beat-up, broken down piece of junk. If you have the know-how to help me get what I am looking for, you should be able to show me how you got what you were looking for. Knowledge without production is like faith without works. James 2:17–18 says, "Even so faith, if it hath not works, is dead, being alone. Yea, a man may say, Thou hast faith, and I have works: shew me thy faith without thy works, and I will shew thee my faith by my works."

Practice what you preach and preach only what you practice!

Checking yourself, your home situation, and your close relatives and friends before witnessing to others is commanded of man by God in Christ in Acts 1:8, as noted above. Also, it is commanded by Jesus in Matthew 28:19–20: "Go ye therefore, and teach all nations, baptizing them in the name of the Father and of the Son, and of the Holy Ghost: Teaching them to observe all things whatsoever I have commanded you: and lo, I am with you always, even unto the end of the world. Amen."

You should know the answers to the following from the previous chapter!

1. Who is known to accuse the brethren?
   _____

2. Where does it say Satan tempts the Christian?
   _____

3. What Scripture says, "He tries to take the Christian captive at his will"?

   _____

4. What book details Satan's desire to hinder the Christian in his work for the Lord?

   _____

4

If You Can't See, Turn on the Light!

The Lamp of the Body!

Jesus said, "The lamp of the body is the eye. "If your eye is pure, there will be sunshine in your soul. But if your eye is clouded with evil thoughts and desires, you are in deep spiritual darkness. And oh, how deep that darkness can be" (Matt. 6:22–23, TLB).

The search to see ourselves as we really are and as we are seen by others obviously begins with seeing. As elementary as that may sound, nonetheless, it is an absolute truth. In fact, this observation is crucial to this investigation. Proper evaluation begins with seeing things properly. Seeing things properly begins with a clean and unobstructed view. Example, a microscope with obstructions (dirt, grime, or grease) on the lens will obstruct or blur any view.

Similarly, Jesus says, this often happens to the body. "The eye is the lamp of the body," therefore the eye should not be obstructed by any impediment, but be clean and clear to receive the right picture. It cannot be obstructed and yield clear vision. The importance of "seeing" is reflected in that the word is used 796 times in the New International Version of the Bible, such as Psalm 119:18 ("Open my eyes, that I may see wondrous things from your law") and Proverbs 26:12 ("Do you see a man wise in his own eyes? There is more hope for a fool than for him").

As each chapter unfolds, take note of the many obstructions that need examining or removing in order to see properly. The text says, "The human eye gives light to the body so it can make careful choices in where and how to walk." This means that your spiritual vision affects how you view everything around you, including yourselves. The ability to see properly affects who you are, how you walk, talk and what you do with your lives.

Verse 22 says, "If therefore your eye is clear" (the Greek word for clear is *haplous*, meaning "simple or single or seeing whole and undivided"). Then from that, sound and healthy use of the eye will follow. Here's the basic thought: single clear vision versus double vision, understanding that double vision is blurred vision. Verse 23 says. "But if your eye is bad to start with ["Bad" is *poneros*, meaning:(a) in the physical sense, in poor condition, sick, and (b) in the ethical sense, worthless, evil and bad], it will infect and reflect the whole body."

Clear vision then, or spiritual understanding as given by the Word and the Holy Spirit gives the ability to recognize the true values of life or what is important or frivolous. Thus avoiding the waste of evil perspectives and distortions of the world. If what Oscar Wilde said in his day was true, it is even more so today. He said, "Nowadays people know the price of everything and the value of nothing." It is these true values that gives one the capacity to make value choices, beginning with the vision of self. This lack of vision and values is reflected in the great increase of the "woes" (tragedies) in the world.

If man's vision is clear, then the whole of his life will be full of light and insight. He will have the ability, the wisdom, the desire, and the will to make wise choices in life. But if man's vision is evil, which means he'll either have false vision, or double vision (divided vision), then his life will be flooded with darkness and untruths. Anything divided is a detriment. "But Jesus knew their thoughts, and said to them: Every kingdom divided against itself is brought to desolation, and every city or house divided against itself will not stand" (Matt. 12:25). This is reflective of men and women stumbling around in the dark, going in a completely wrong direction or perpetually trying to go in two directions. Either way, it is an unstable situation, leaving the person unable to fulfill God's purpose for life and ultimately missing being blessed. Remember, a key basic principle of life says, "Outlook determines outcome."

To achieve the proper outlook and in-look, the first step necessary (though admittedly difficult), is to look honestly at oneself. Lying and deception combined with irrational thinking and selfish viewing will not help get to where he/she needs to be. Or shall I say, where one must be in order to be at ones best and be blessed by God. Note the warnings of God for honesty with ourselves.

1 John 1:8, says, "If we say that we have no sin, we are deceiving ourselves and the truth is not in us."

Note: If we say, before Christ's blood has cleansed us, we have no sin, we lie. To be cleansed from; or if, even after we have experienced the cleansing virtue of his blood, and are acquitted through the merit of it from all past guilt, and saved from all evil tempers, words, and works; "if, we say we have no sin we lie."

Even after cleansing, justification, regeneration, and sanctification, we say we have no sin, and say we are perfectly sinless, and that our spirit and conduct can bear the scrutiny of God's holiness and justice, as exhibited in his spiritual and holy law; we still deceive ourselves. The point being a capital offence that the truth is not in us, neither in our mouth nor in our heart.

Psalm 36:1–4 is evidence:

> Transgression speaks to the ungodly within his heart; there is no fear of God before his eyes. For it flatters him in his own eyes concerning the discovery of his iniquity and the hatred of it. The words of his mouth are wickedness and deceit; He has ceased to be wise and to do good."

In short: here's the message from God concerning the sinfulness of the wicked: the wicked have lost the fear of God. In their eyes, they flatter themselves too much to detect or hate their sin. The words of their mouths are wicked and deceitful; they fail to act wisely or do good. They plot trouble while on their beds; they set themselves in a way that is not good and do not reject evil.

Seeking more information on the subject, see also Jeremiah 2:34–35. Jeremiah said :

> Also on your skirts is found the lifeblood of the innocent poor; you did not find them breaking in. But in spite of all these things, yet you said, "I am innocent; surely His anger is turned away from me." Behold, I will enter into judgment with you because you say, "I have not sinned."

> The heart is more deceitful than all else and desperately sick; who can understand it? I, the Lord, search the heart, I test the mind, even to give to each man according to his ways, according to the results of is deeds. (Jer. 17:9–10)

> Or do you not know that the unrighteous will not inherit the kingdom of God? Do not be deceived; neither fornicators, nor idolaters, nor adulterers, nor effeminate, nor homosexuals, nor thieves, nor the covetous, nor drunkards, nor revilers, nor swindlers, will inherit the kingdom of God. (1 Cor. 6:9–10)

Galatians 6:3 reminds, "If a man think himself to be something, when he is nothing, he deceiveth himself." Make note, Satan is the great deceiver. In fact, Genesis 3 notes that when people follow Satan they need reminding of his subtle (deceptive) nature. Genesis 3:1 says, "Now the serpent was more subtil than any beast of the field which the LORD God had made. And he said unto the woman, yea, hath God said, ye shall not eat of every tree of the garden?"

> The deceptive serpent said to the woman, "You surely will not die! For God knows that in the day you eat from it your eyes will be opened, and you will be like God, knowing good and evil." (Gen. 3:4–5)

> You are of your father the devil, and you want to do the desires of your father He was a murderer from the beginning, and does not stand in the truth because there is no truth in him Whenever he speaks a lie, he speaks from his own nature, for he is a liar and the father of lies. (John 8:44)

> But I am afraid that, as the serpent deceived Eve by his craftiness, your minds will be led astray from the simplicity and purity of devotion to Christ. (2 Cor. 11:3)

God commands us to be honest with ourselves, acknowledging God already knows what we can be and who we should be. He created us. Psalm 8 and Hebrews 2:6–8 remind us, "But one in a certain place testified, saying, what is man, that thou art mindful of him? or the son of man, that thou visitest him? Thou madest him a little lower than the angels; thou crowned him with glory and honor, and didst set him over the works of thy hands: Thou hast put all things in subjection under his feet. For in that he put all in subjection under him, he left nothing *that is* not put under him. But now we see not yet all things put under him."

If mankind understands and accepts their God-given position (as dominant dresser, keeper, and manager of creation), for which clearly God made man. Any who doubt this only need to read Genesis 2:15. It further substantiates (NASB), "Then the Lord God took the man and put him into the Garden of Eden to cultivate it and keep it." Any valid search for self-awareness forces the acknowledgement of our capabilities and our faults. It's counterproductive to overlook either.

Acknowledge them both makes me stronger, not weaker. A fighter who does not acknowledge his weakness cannot steer the fight to his strengths and will never reach his full potential. If he acknowledges for example, his chin is weak and he cannot take a punch; his winning strategy must incorporate minimizing getting hit. If he refuse to acknowledge this weakness, instead of the commentators saying, there he goes, they will say, there he lay. God warns mankind in Galatians 6:3, "For if a man think himself to be something, when he is nothing, he deceives himself." Acknowledge who and what you are. Proverbs 26:12 says, "See you a man wise in his own conceit? There is more hope of a fool than of him."

In other words, there is more hope for fools than for people who think they are wise. Luke 18:11 records Jesus: "The Pharisee stood by himself and prayed:'God, I thank you that I am not like other people—robbers, evildoers, adulterers—or even like this tax collector. But after the prayer he went home unjustified and empty. The Pharisee's mistake was that he did not pray to God, but prayed to himself. He thanked God that he was not like other humans. He thought he was better. Thus his prayer received attention, but the wrong kind from God. In 1 Corinthians 3:18, it says, "Let no one deceive himself. If any of you thinks he is wise in the ways of this world, he must become a fool to become really wise." In 1 Corinthians 8:2, it says, "And if any man think that he knoweth anything, he knoweth nothing, yet as he ought to know."

It's clear, to perform with God-blessed efficiency, one must acknowledge who and what he is totally, which includes acknowledgement of faults and weaknesses. Even when our faults makes us look shameful, ignorant, guilty or failures, reality demands that we deal honestly with them. The main reason for my acceptance of these facts is the knowledge that deep down all humanity has faults. Ecclesiastes 7:20 says, "Indeed, there is not a righteous man on earth who continually does good and who never sins."

Isaiah 53:6 says, "All we like sheep have gone astray; we have turned everyone to his own way." Romans 3:23 reminds, "For all have sinned, and come short of the glory of God." Romans 3:10 says, "As it is written, There is none righteous, no, not one." In 1 John 1:8–10, it says, "If we say that we have no sin, we are deceiving ourselves and the truth is not in us.

If we confess our sins, He is faithful and righteous to forgive us our sins and to cleanse us from all unrighteousness. If we say that we have not sinned, we make Him a liar and His word is not in us."

If Mirrows Could Talk!

> For if anyone is a hearer of the word and not a doer, he is like a man who looks intently at his natural face in a mirror. For he looks at himself and goes away and at once forgets what he was like. (James 1:23–24, NIV)

This is a great place to get a pen and a piece of paper. Stand in front of a mirror and write down what you see. Look carefully and honestly at your characteristics, both inward (mentally and spiritually) and outward (physically). I mean, totally examine yourself, especially emotionally and spiritually. For instance, physically, look at how you stand. Are you standing straight, with a serious, confident, "mean what I say" look, or are slouched over in fear, talking, but not saying nothing?

Are you appearing bashful and afraid to even gaze eye to eye at your own self? If you are, you need to acknowledge this fear. This foretells something about you. It displays how you view yourself and subsequently, how the world views you. Appearing unsure, insecure, and afraid to look at yourself in the face is bad enough. But you need to know that it carries over and is certainly not the portrayal God wants from you, the managers and caretakers of the earth (Gen. 2:15).

One of the first great steps towards achieving the goal of self-awareness and confidence is acknowledgement of this truth: "Appearances do matter, and you don't get a second chance to make a first impression." After all, Jesus said, "To the Jews who had believed him, if you hold to my teaching, you are really my disciples. Then you will know the truth, and the truth will make you free" (John 8:31–32).

Additionally, while standing in front of the mirror, don't just examine your looks and stature physically, but examine your mental state as well. Talk to yourself and listen to yourself. Admit your weaknesses and shortcomings. If you are not patient with people or don't like being around people, particularly children, etc., own it and write those observations down. From time to time, take a look at them. If you are moving in the right direction, there should be less and less of these negatives and more good qualities added to your list.

Following this advice is a great beginning on your journey toward improvement. If you cannot acknowledge your weaknesses, errors, and failures to yourself, you will never admit them to anyone else, thus hindering the progress toward becoming your best and being blessed by God, which you and I know is a great desire of our hearts. Only a foolish person does not want to be blessed by God "from whom all blessings flow." The doxologist sang, "Praise God, from Whom all blessings flow; Praise Him, all creatures here below; Praise Him above, ye heavenly host; Praise Father, Son, and Holy Ghost."

Go ahead and begin. Get into the closet of your mind and start recording and replaying your thoughts. While doing that, remember Paul's list in Galatians 5:17–21 and 1 Cor. 6:8–10: "selfish, hateful, rude, mean, manipulative, arrogant, controlling, sexual immoral, impure, sensual, idol worshippers, have enmity (full of animosity), jealous, angry, rivals, dissentful, divided, envious, heavy drinkers (or drunks), drug addicts, lovers of porn, orgies, open marriages and things like these." Specifically note 1 Cor. 6:8–10, "No, you yourselves do wrong and cheat, and you do these things to your brethren! Do you not know that the unrighteous will not inherit the kingdom of God? Do not be deceived. Neither fornicators, nor idolaters, nor adulterers, nor homosexuals, nor sodomites, nor thieves, nor covetous, nor drunkards, nor revilers, nor extortionists will inherit the kingdom of God."

Hopefully, the first lesson learned is to admit your mistakes and weaknesses. Write them down and pray over them one at a time. Continue making plans how to correct them and then go to work activating them. Each day—or however long it takes to overcome the issue—come back and check it off of the list one at time. I am praying for your success. Remember: "Faith without works is dead, being alone" (James 2:14).

Write down some of your weaknesses:

_____

_____

_____

_____

5

Let This Mind Be in You

> Let this mind be in you, which was also in Christ Jesus: Who, being in the form of God, thought it not robbery to be equal with God: But made himself of no reputation, and took upon him the form of a servant, and was made in the likeness of men: And being found in fashion as a man, he humbled himself, and became obedient unto death, even the death of the cross. (Phil. 2:5)

Make note of how you respond to others around you.

As Christ humbled himself, humble and examine yourself. Within the last few hours, days, weeks, and months, have you been encouraging to others or discouraging? Think about your last conversation. Was every word or even every other word out of your mouth an attack or antidote? Were your responses driven by fear (either identified or an unidentified reluctance), jealousy, envy, or some other insecurity? Keep reminding yourself of the task at hand and the fact that "truth makes you free" (John 8:32), a fact that even the legal system recognizes. The clerk of court makes you swear on the Bible that you will "tell the truth, the whole truth, and nothing but the truth."

If you want to be your best and be blessed by God, start seeing yourself! Note Paul's testimony to King Agrippa. Acts 26:17–18 says, "Rescuing you from the Jewish people and from the Gentiles, to whom I am sending you. To open their eyes so that they may turn from darkness to light and from the dominion of Satan to God, that they may receive forgiveness of sins and an inheritance among those who have been sanctified by faith in Me."

The reward of Christ will be well worth the effort! If every person in civilization could see themselves as they really are, the world would be more of what God intended. Literally, there could be peace, even paradise, on earth. Even before the birth of Christ, there was a search for peace. But at his birth, the angel revealed God's quest for mankind. He said, "Glory to God in the highest, and on earth peace, good will toward men" (Luke 2:14). This is just one of the many reasons Jesus came. Here is a list of a few of the other significant ones:

1. He came to die.

> From that time Jesus began to show to His disciples that He must go to Jerusalem, and suffer many things from the elders and chief priests and scribes, and be killed, and be raised the third day. (Matt. 16:21)

I believe the number 1 reason why Jesus came to the earth and was born a man was so that he could die. Did you know that it is impossible to kill God? God is a supreme spiritual power, and it is impossible to eliminate God from existence. But that does not mean that God as a man could not die a normal physical death. It is pretty obvious that Jesus proved that after hanging on the cross.

2. He came to save sinners.

> And Jesus said unto him, This day is salvation come to this house, for so much as he also is a son of Abraham. For the Son of man is come to seek and to save that which was lost. (Luke 19:10)

> For God so loved the world, that he gave his only begotten Son, that whosoever believeth in him should not perish, but have everlasting life. (John 3:16)

I believe the number 2 reason Jesus came to this planet in a physical form was so that He could save us. Like everyone else, we have all sinned and come short of the glory of God (Rom 3:23). Even though we are not really worthy of salvation, God chose to save us anyway.

3. He came to undo the works of the devil!

> He that committeth sin is of the devil; for the devil sinneth from the beginning. For this purpose the Son of God was manifested, that he might destroy the works of the devil. (1 John 3:8)

I hope that you do understand who the devil is. I hope you also understand that Satan is not on God's payroll and does not work for God. You see, God has the power to tell Satan what to do, but yet is this the way God is? Is God pulling all of the strings in heaven and causing everything in the world to happen exactly like He wants it to happen? I do not think so. You do understand that the Sovereign God is able to give man free will by His choice and design? If you do not understand that man has a free will, you do not understand that it was you that chose to get out of bed this morning and not God.

4. Jesus came and died so that the Holy Spirit could come and abide!

> Nevertheless I tell you the truth. It is expedient for you that I go away, for if I go not away, the Comforter will not come unto you; but if I depart, I will send Him unto you. (John 16:9)

This truth is simple but yet very important to understand. Without Jesus's death, we would not have the Holy Spirit living inside us today. Of course, the Holy Spirit is only in those who have received Him and not in everyone. God does not force His entrance into the spirits of anyone. Here is a verse of scripture that tells us something that Jesus said to us personally:

> And I will pray the Father, and he shall give you another Comforter, that he may abide with you forever. (John 14:16)

Jesus came to install these and others. These were designed by God to reduce confrontation, conflict, and devastation. If each person could see himself for himself and correct his/her own errors, what a joyous and peaceful place the world would become. It would be a worthwhile effort. It could also remove guns; for far too many people use them against each other.

I know the argument for Second Amendment Rights. But I also know every person has right to live out their lives freely without fear of getting shot by the bearers of guns and weaponry. Wikipedia, the free encyclopedia, reports that gun violence in the United States results in thousands of deaths and thousands more injuries annually:

"According to the Centers for Disease Control and Prevention, in 2013, firearms (excluding BB and pellet guns) were used in 84,258 nonfatal injuries (26.65 per 100,000 US citizens) and 11,208 deaths by homicide (3.5 per 100,000), 21,175 by suicide with a firearm., 505 deaths due to accidental discharge of a firearm, and 281 deaths due to firearms-use with "undetermined intent" for a total of 33,169 deaths related to firearms (excluding firearm deaths due to legal (intervention)."

If the people of the earth would accept God's Word and my advice and look at themselves and truly see themselves with all of their weaknesses and evil tendencies, violence and confrontation will greatly diminish. There would be no need for gun packing (deer and rabbits don't attack humans in the streets, for those carrying guns claiming hunting as their reason). Thus, there is real potential for guns and violence to be eradicated and become a condition of the past. The mass shooting tragedies occurring in America every minute could cease.

If people would take the time to look inward more and less outward, the world would be a better place to live. Clearly God created us with the capacity; just look at the structure of the hand. When you point at other's faults, more fingers are pointed at you than at them. What a wonderful thought! What a great possibility! What a marvelous dream! It is one well worth searching for. If people could see themselves, each person could resolve his/her own issues. In order for this to have a chance of happening, here are some principle steps that need taking:

The first step recommended is Christianity (Christ likeness).

How does one achieve Christianity?

1. Study the Bible to strengthen your conviction that it is the inspired word of God. If you want to be a Christian based on what the Bible says, it is an absolute necessity to know what it says, believe what it says, and do what it says. But before you can do, know, and believe, what it says, you have to study it. The evidence of this is recorded in 2 Timothy 2:15, when the apostle Paul says, "Study to show thyself approved unto God, a workman that needeth not to be ashamed, rightly dividing the word of truth." So does King David in Psalm 109:18. He said, "Thy word is a lamp unto my feet, and a light unto my path."

    The reason the Word is so important and necessary is that God is the author and God Himself inspired each and every word written. In 2 Timothy 3:16–17, it says, "All scripture is given by inspiration of God, and is profitable for doctrine, for reproof, for correction, for instruction in righteousness: that the man of God may be perfect, thoroughly furnished unto all good works." If you want to be better and headed toward perfection (Christian maturity), the first step is to study the Bible (Basic Instruction Before Leaving Earth).

2. Repent of sin or wrongdoing, whether known or unknown. Jesus said, "Unless you 'repent'[change your mind, feel sorrow for your actions and turn around], you will all likewise perish" (Luke 13:2,5). Repent means you must "change your way of thinking"

and "turn away from your old ways to Christ's way." Jesus said, "I am the Way, the truth and the life, and no man comest to the Father, except by me" (John 14:6).

3. Be born again. John 3:1–8 says,

> Now there was a man of the Pharisees named Nicodemus, a ruler of the Jews. This man came to Jesus by night and said to him, "Rabbi, we know that you are a teacher come from God, for no one can do these signs that you do unless God is with him. Jesus answered him, truly, truly, I say to you, unless one is born again he cannot see the kingdom of God. Nicodemus said to him, "How can a man be born when he is old? Can he enter a second time into his mother's womb and be born?" Jesus answered, "Truly, truly, I say to you, unless one is born of water and the Spirit, he cannot enter the kingdom of God. That which is born of the flesh is flesh, and that which is born of the Spirit is spirit. Do not marvel that I said to you, 'You must be born again. The wind blows where it wishes, and you hear its sound, but you do not know where it comes from or where it goes. So it is with everyone who is born of the Spirit."

   To be born again, just remember the ABCs of religion: *acknowledge* God, *believe* in Jesus, and *confess* your sin and repent of them.

4. Believe and be baptized. Acts 2:37–38 says, "Now when they heard this, they were pricked in their heart, and said unto Peter and to the rest of the apostles, Men and brethren, what shall we do? Then Peter said unto them, Repent, and be baptized every one of you in the name of Jesus Christ for the remission of sins, and ye shall receive the gift of the Holy Ghost."

   The great commission of Matthew 28:19–20 says, "Go ye therefore, and teach all nations, baptizing them in the name of the Father, and of the Son, and of the Holy Ghost: Teaching them to observe all things whatsoever I have commanded you: and, lo, I am with you always, even unto the end of the world. Amen." "Be baptized in the name of the Father, the Son and the Holy Ghost," as some believe, that means "in Jesus name" (John 3:5).

5. Be filled with the Holy Ghost.

> Do you not know, that as many of us as were baptized into Jesus Christ were baptized into His death? Therefore we are buried with Him by baptism into death: that as Christ was raised up from the dead by the glory of the Father, even so we also should walk in newness of life. For if we have been planted together [in baptism] in the likeness of His death, we shall be also be in the likeness of His resurrection: Knowing this, that our old man is crucified with Him, that the body of sin might be destroyed, that henceforth we should not serve sin. For he that is dead is freed from sin. (Rom 6:3–7)

After being born again, begin the journey toward Christianity. As Paul says, men and women must grow from infancy to childhood to adulthood and to mature Christianity. It is here that one can really begin to see himself for himself. It is here that one can achieve success through Christian maturity. Christian maturity involves, incorporates, and activates the commands of God in the life of the Christian.

In 1 Corinthians 3:1–3, Paul outlines this journey, beginning as "babes in Christ." He says, "And I, brethren, could not speak unto you as unto spiritual, but as unto carnal, even as unto babes in Christ. I have fed you with milk, and not with meat: for hitherto ye were not able to bear it, neither yet now are ye able. For ye are yet carnal: for whereas there is among you envying, and strife, and divisions, are ye not carnal, and walk as men?"

The goal laid out by Paul for Christians was to not drink milk but to eat meat, representing growth in Christian principles, works, and faith. Consider this question: Within the world that we live in today, as violent as it is, do you think mature Christianity can be achieved? Think about it honestly for a few minutes. I hope you answered yes. In fact, this is God's goal for man: to be mature in Christianity and go far and beyond the norms of society.

Jesus said, "For if you love those who love you, what reward do you have? Do not even the tax collectors [sinners] do the same? And if you greet only your own people, what are you doing more than others? Do not even pagans do that? Therefore, be perfect, as your heavenly Father is perfect" (Matt. 5:46–48). The word "perfect" is rendered mature in the Greek language.

Christian maturity incorporates salvation first, then love and productivity second. Love is the mark of Christianity. It has been said that no love, no Christianity: Little love, little Christianity: Much love, much Christianity. In fact, in John 13:34–35, Jesus said, "A new commandment I give unto you, that ye love one another; as I have loved you, that ye also love one another. By this shall all men know that ye are my disciples, if ye have love one to another."

In 1 John 4:7–8, it says, "Beloved, let us love one another: for love is of God; and every one that loveth is born of God, and knoweth God. He that loveth not, knoweth not God; for God is love." Love is the first fruit of the Spirit. Galatians 5:22–23 says, "But the fruit of the Spirit is love, joy, peace, longsuffering, gentleness, goodness, faith, Meekness, temperance: against such there is no law." A deeper understanding of love will be addressed later in the book.

In John 10:10, Jesus says, "The thief comest for to steal, kill and to destroy, but I am come that you might life and have it more abundantly." Mark 2:17 says, "When Jesus heard it, he saith unto them, They that are whole have no need of the physician, but they that are sick: I came not to call the righteous, but sinners to repentance."

A great step toward achieving abundant living is for men and women "Accept Christ as Savior, grow in love and production. This is necessary, if mankind is to see themselves as they really are and become better and blessed by God." If you acknowledge this possibility, it is a great step of achievement. I have and am totally convinced of its truth. In fact, it is the motivation and will for the expense of time, money, and effort to write this book.

Learn from Jesus! He turns the light on Himself!

Jesus's exploration of human relationships and self-evaluation in Matthew 7 reveals his views on justice, fairness, and honesty. Before pinpointing procedures and principles and before dotting any i's and crossing any t's, first, Jesus emphasized humanity's need for self-examination and self-control. Galatians 6:4 says, "But each one must examine his own work, and then he will have reason for boasting in regard to himself alone, and not in regard to another." In 2 Cor. 13:5, it says, "Test yourselves to see if you are in the faith; examine yourselves!"

Second; after self-examination, Jesus's emphasized people's need to acknowledge their own status and standing then activate their findings. What does that mean? It means that "people should practice what they preach and testify (in living) what they teach." It means that the people rendering judgments or decisions on the lives of others are to look first at their own situations seriously, honestly, and totally.

They are to ask themselves, "What would I do or say if this was my predicament?" Or more poignantly, WWJD (What would Jesus do?) and then make the proper judgments and recommendations. The words of a song go "There are too many people trying to take care of other people's business, and they can't even take care of their own. What they need to do is take six months to mind their own business and six months to leave other folks' business alone. Sweep around your own front door before you try to sweep around mine."

Once the process of sweeping around your own front door has been completed, make note of the biblical reflections. The Bible says, "How you judge and render decisions on the actions of others, ultimately, God will render the same measure of justice to you and your actions." Jesus asked, "Why do you look at the speck of sawdust in your brother's eye and pay no attention to the plank in your own eye? How can you say to your brother, 'Let me take the speck out of your eye,' when all the time there is a plank in your own eye? 5 You hypocrite, first take the plank out of your own eye, and then you will see clearly to remove the speck from your brother's eye" (Matt. 7:5, NIV).

What a wonderful world this could become if people possessed the ability to see themselves as they are and how they are seen by others. Hopefully your understanding has increased and now you are able to see the potential of the premise, which is to exhort men and women to seek their rightful place in creation and to set its tone and direction and revolutionize the world. Think about the world's capability and potential to resolve conflicting interactions and the peace that could be found if humans could see their own flaws and errors. Just the thought of self-correction gives me chills as I think about the possibility of actually possessing heaven on earth.

Think about the huge decline of arguments, confrontations, and conflicts. Words of criticism, correction, rebuke, and chastisement would greatly be lessened, if not totally eradicated. Just the thought of people living without the correction of others, except under training and teaching purposes, gives me chills and thrills. Not to mention the change in people's character where there would no longer be a need to defend selfish positions and personal agendas. One would not only see themselves but would have the ability and will to correct oneself. This would galvanize humanity and be a great step socially toward real civilization.

Sounds revolutionary, doesn't it? I know, but what a thought. Take another step further. What if all people across the globe could see themselves and correct themselves? The extinction of war (the state of hostility, conflict, and antagonism among mankind.) could be a real possibility. The thought of a world without war, with no more innocent young people being killed and maimed, brings tears to my eyes. Revolutionary, yes, but it could happen.

Now that the dire consequences of negativity have been explored, let us look at where we are versus where we should be and how to get there. In the next chapter, these inquiries will be investigated. But before moving on from this chapter, answer the following:

How does one achieve Christianity?

1. What was number 1?

   _____

2. What was number 2?

   _____

3. What was number 3?

   _____

4. What was number 4?

   _____

5. What was number 5?

   _____

6

Man's Dilemma

> Then one of them, which was a lawyer, asked him a question, tempting him, and saying, Master, which is the great commandment in the law? Jesus said unto him, Thou shalt love the Lord thy God with all thy heart, and with all thy soul, and with all thy mind. This is the first and great commandment. And the second *is* like unto it, Thou shalt love thy neighbor as thyself. On these two commandments hang all the law and the prophets. (Matt. 22:35–40)

The text is a crystal clear revelation from the Lord of an extremely important fact. Innately, men and women love themselves. (*Innate* means something created before birth within the human biology of each member.) In this case, innateness protects, provides, and preserves each human's interests. Both personal experience and history teaches that this built-in prejudicial action doesn't have to be taught to humans. Automatically or instinctively, it comes in the birth box of every normal person. As instinctively as babies cry to reveal a discomfort and desire for selfish attention, human beings display innate tendencies.

Without this innate instinct (or prejudice, if you will) for self-promotion and self-survival, humans are diagnosed with a variety of dysfunctional ailments. Self-harm, self-mutilation, and self-injury are some of the mental health issues treated everyday as an attempt to restore innate normality of human life.

Here's just a brief example to prove and enhance this point. The most extreme abnormality to self-survival is suicide. According to the Thursday, September 18, 2014 *New York Times* article of Health Guide: Suicide is considered a disorder. It further notes reasons for suicide. Suicidal behaviors usually occur in people with one or more of the following:

- Bipolar disorder

- Borderline personality disorder
- Depression
- Drug or alcohol dependence
- Schizophrenia
- Stressful life issues, such as serious financial or relationship problems

People who try to commit suicide are often trying to get away from life situations that seem to them too impossible to deal with. Many who make such a suicide attempt seek relief from the following:

- Feeling ashamed, guilty, or a burden to others.
- Feeling like a victim.
- Feelings of rejection, loss, or loneliness

Suicidal behaviors may occur when there is a situation or event that the person finds overwhelming, such as the following:

- Aging (the elderly have the highest rate of suicide)
- Death of a loved one
- Dependence on drugs or alcohol
- Emotional trauma
- Serious physical illness
- Unemployment or money problems.

As suicide is the result of abnormality and dysfunction, so is the lack of prejudice (the strong desire) for one's own survival and promotion. Prejudice has been given a bad name because of discrimination (race, age, sex, religion, etc.), which is evil and wrong. But prejudice as defined is both natural and normal for humans to have. Having said that quickly, let it be said clearly that though normal and natural to possess prejudice, it is evil and immature Christianity to act upon because of race, age, religion, or sex (e.g., discriminating against women in a male dominant society).

Romans 8:7 (God's Word translation) says, "Carnal-mindedness is so because of the corrupt nature (of mankind) and has a hostile attitude toward God. It refuses to place itself under the authority of God's standards because it can't without God's help." So for the Christian, prejudice (or selfish pride of flesh) must be acknowledged and controlled. This is a key theme of this book.

The Christian disciple learning to be Christ-like must deny himself, take up his cross, and follow Jesus (Matt. 16:24). Remember the story of Snow White. It sheds light on the predicament in which mankind finds itself. It is a great example and highlights the necessity of the theme of this book to the world. According to Wikipedia, the story goes as follows:

> At the beginning of the story of Snow White, a queen sits sewing at an open window during a winter snowfall. She pricks her finger with her needle, causing three drops of blood to fall onto the snow and on the ebony window frame.
>
> Admiring the beauty of the resulting color combination, the Queen says to herself: "Oh, how I wish, I had a daughter as white as snow, as red as blood, and as black as that wood of the window frame." Soon after, indeed, the queen gives birth to a baby girl as white as snow, as red as blood and with hair as black as ebony. She named her Snow White and not long after, the queen dies.
>
> Years later, the King takes a new wife, who was beautiful but also unutterably wicked and vain. The new Queen possessed a Magic Mirror which she asked every morning: "Magic mirror in my hand, who is the fairest in that land?" The mirror always replies: "My Queen, you are the fairest in that land." The Queen was always pleased with that, because the magic mirror never lied.
>
> But, when Snow White reached the age of seven, she became as beautiful as a bright sunny day and even more beautiful than the Queen. Now when the Queen asked her mirror, "Magic mirror in my hand, who is the fairest in that land?" It responded: "My Queen, you are the fairest here so true. But Snow White is a thousand times more beautiful than you."
>
> The mirror's reply sent the queen into shock. She became yellow and green with envy and jealousy, and from that hour her heart turned against Snow White. With every day that passed, she hated Snow White more and more. Envy and pride, like ill weeds, grow taller in her heart every day, leaving her with no peace day or night. The Queen ordered a huntsman to take Snow White into the deepest woods to be

killed. As proof of her death, the queen demanded the huntsman to produce Snow White's lungs and liver.

As ordered, the huntsman took Snow White into the forest. After raising his knife, he found himself unable to kill her as she sobbed heavily. She begged him: "Oh, dear huntsman, please don't kill me! Leave me with my life, I will run into the forest and never come back!" Convinced that the young girl would be eaten alive by some hungry animal, the huntsman left her behind alive. Instead of bringing the lungs and liver of Snow White, he brought the Queen the lungs and liver of a young boar; which the cook prepared for consumption by the Queen.

The queen's desire to be beautiful was not an issue or was wrong in and of itself. But her desire was not only to be beautiful but to be the most beautiful woman in the land. Like the meal prepared by the cook that she consumed, this desire for beauty consumed her. Her desire to be more than what she was and the inability to see herself as she was led her to murder. Although her murderous plot to kill Snow White failed, she did all she could.

When the Queen looked in the mirror, she did not really see herself. She saw only what she wanted to see, which was her beauty; and that misguided view led to tragedy and despair.

The Danger of Improper Perception

Unfortunately the queen's failure is repeated too often. People's failure to properly and accurately see themselves leads to disaster and despair. Within the pages of Matthew 16, Jesus addressed the issue of improper perception. He spent three to three and a half years teaching and preaching to the disciples. As he neared the end of his earthly ministry, he was concerned about the disciples' perception of him and just having proper vision altogether.

Mark 8:22–26 notes,

> They came to Bethsaida, and some people brought a blind man and begged Jesus to touch him. He took the blind man by the hand and led him outside the village. When he had spit on the man's eyes and put his hands on him, Jesus asked, "Do you see anything?" He looked up and said, "I see people and they look like trees walking around." Once more Jesus put his hands on the man's eyes. Then his eyes were

opened, his sight was restored, and he saw everything clearly. Jesus sent him home, saying, "Don't even go into the village."

Obviously, improper perception concerned Jesus greatly, so much so that he made sure, the disciples viewed him correctly. Notice the next few verses. Peter properly perceived Jesus and declared his messiah-ship!

> Jesus and his disciples went on to the villages around Caesarea Philippi. On the way he asked them, "Who do people say I am? They replied, "Some say John the Baptist; others say Elijah; and still others, one of the prophets." But what about you, he asked? "Who do you say I am?" Peter answered, "You are the Messiah." Jesus warned them not to tell anyone about him. (Mark 8:27–30)

The above was Mark's version of events. But Matthew 16:13–20 gives much more needed background information of Jesus's concern for the disciples' perception. Matthew names the place, the time of day, and other specific information needed for their final exam. Matthew says that Jesus paused at Caesarea Philippi and gave them preparatory questions.

It needs noting that the region of Caesarea Philippi (v. 13a, a city so named to distinguish it from the coastal Caesarea) was largely Gentile territory. This time the context revealed that Jesus came not to evangelize Gentiles (as he had in Matt. 15:21–39) but to withdraw from the Jewish leadership (Matt. 16:1) and the crowds for a time of instruction.

As Matthew 16:13 and 15 indicate, by this stage of the ministry, both the crowd and the disciples had seen and heard him many times with different conclusions being drawn about Him. The question of verse 13, the "people" referred to the Jewish population. Note that Matthew's questions concerns "the Son of Man" in Mark 8:27 and Luke 9:18). However, Matthew 16:13 refers to Jesus personally as "the Son of Man." Immediately thereafter, Jesus moved directly to the question and asked the disciples, "Who do you say I am?" (16:15). How do you see me?

They replied, "Some of the people say you are John the Baptist; others say, Elijah; and still others, Jeremiah or one of the prophets" (16:14). The first view refers to that of Herod Antipas (Matt. 14:2). The second attaches Jesus to the role of forerunner, instead of John the Baptist (Matt. 11:10–14). While the Synoptic gospels mention "the prophets," generally, only Matthew refers specifically to him being Jeremiah. All these ascriptions express great respect for Jesus, but none are adequate in response to what Jesus's ministry entailed and who he really was and is.

Hardly much has changed. As it was then, so it is today: truth and reality needs to be understood and accepted. While the saying "perception is everything" means much, it doesn't hold true in all cases, and this is one of them. Perception as defined is the act or faculty of perceiving, or apprehending by means of the senses or of the mind; cognition; understanding. C. W. Leadbeater said, "It is one of the most common of mistakes to consider that the limit of our power of perception is also the limit of all there is to perceive."

Thus, perception itself is perplex. Among its problems are inaccuracy and nonbenefit. It's clear in Jesus's discussion with the disciples that their perception was not reality. They did not see Jesus clearly or accurately. However, Jesus knew the importance of accurate information and proper perception. Exegesis reports, this to be the reason for the detour and temporary retreat at Caesarea Philippi. It was crucial for all of the disciples to be on the same page of perception. They needed to see Jesus for who and what he really is. The same is still true today. It's needed greatly for people to see properly and this perception of reality begins with knowledge of the real Jesus of Nazareth.

Just a Couple More Things!

Jesus's Understanding of Himself

What He said about Himself!

To help clear up a major mistake of history by so many denominations, the central figure of the passage Matthew 16:18–19 was not Peter. It was Jesus. What Jesus says about Peter being a rockmust be viewed in the light of what Jesus says about himself.

His authority. It is Jesus that utters the words in verses 17–19. "He answered and said to Peter, Blessed are you, Simon Bar-Jonah, for flesh and blood has not revealed this to you, but My Father who is in heaven. And I also say to you that you are Peter, and on this rock I will build my church, and the gates of Hades shall not prevail against it. And I will give you the keys of the kingdom of heaven, and whatever you bind on earth will be bound in heaven, and whatever you loose on earth will be loosed in heaven." As God the Son, Jesus knows that Peter's insight (v. 16) was revealed by God the Father. He knew, earthly decisions get their power from heaven (v. 19).

In consequence of the Father's revelation as to who Jesus really is, Jesus pronounces Simon the recipient of God's blessing, grants him the name, "Peter," meaning rock," and promises him "the keys to the kingdom." Indicating, whatever Simon Peter is to be and do is the direct effect of Jesus' authoritative declaration upon his life. It needs noting that God gave man this same ruling authority in the Garden of Eden at Creation. Genesis 1:28, says, "And God blessed them, and God said unto them, be fruitful, and multiply, and replenish the earth, and subdue it and have dominion over the fish of the sea, and over the fowl of the air, and over every living thing that moveth upon the earth."

Calamitous Consequences of Improper Perception

The prodigal son of the New Testament (Luke 15) is a great example of the problem of improper perception. He did not see himself and his capabilities as they really were. As played out in the text, had he more understanding about the reality of his success and the real reasons for it, his troubled journey could have been avoided. But because he failed to see himself properly, he was not himself.

The fact that he was not himself is clearly seen in the text. Luke 15:17 says, "And when he came to himself." Thus, he had no real view of reality. His perception was tainted. He did not know who or what he really was. But Jesus said that when he came to his senses and really saw himself and what he had become, first, he examined himself and his situation.

> He said, "How many hired servants of my father's have bread enough and to spare, and I perish with hunger! I will get up and go to my father, and will say to him, 'Father, I have sinned against heaven, and in your sight; I am no longer worthy to be called your son; make me as one of your hired men.'" So he got up and came to his father. But while he was still a long way off, his father saw him and felt compassion for him, and ran and embraced him and kissed him.
>
> The son said to him, "Father, I have sinned against heaven and in your sight; I am no longer worthy to be called your son." But the father said to his servants, "Quickly bring out the best robe and put it on him, and put a ring on his hand and sandals on his feet; and bring the fattened calf, kill it, and let us eat and celebrate; for this son of

mine was dead and has come to life again; he was lost and has been found." And they began to celebrate. (Luke 15:17–24)

This son had messed up completely, and he knew it. He had deserted his family and spent his father's hard-earned money in riotous living. He had no further claim to his forsaken sonship. Legally, his father did not owe him anything physical, mentally, or spiritually. When the son left with everything, he cut all ties to anything of the father.

Yet the son knew his father's love and character. He knew that being his servant was better than being a servant to his heathen employer in a distant country. His heathen employer had placed him the hog's pen and would not even give him the food that the hog's were eating. So he returned back to his father, confessing his sin and hoping for nothing more than to become a hired servant. The father's response was gracious, and he gave the young man what he did not deserve. Thus, the definition of grace: it is giving what is not deserved; and mercy is withholding what is deserved for sin. The consequences of improper perception usually are devastating.

Note that like the prodigal son, after the tragic death of his son, King David knew he did not deserve God's forgiveness or blessings. But unlike the prodigal son, he did not ask God's blessings. He only confessed his sin of adultery and murder. Yet David's repentance resulted in a renewed joy in the presence and service of God and a commitment to teach others to turn from sin. Psalm 51 reveals David's prayer for a renewal of his joy in the Lord (51:8,12). From David's long-lasting relationship with God, there is every reason to believe that he was granted his request.

Additionally note now, David desired to teach others. Specifically, look at Psalm 51:13: "Then I will teach transgressors your ways, and sinners will be converted to you." Now King David will be teaching sinners as a repentant sinner. His goal is to turn sinners from their sin. How different this is from the wicked, who seek to entice others to follow them in their sin: "And although they know the ordinance of God, that those who practice such things are worthy of death, they not only do the same, but also give hearty approval to those who practice them" (Rom. 1:32).

I am reminded of Simon Peter, whose denial our Lord foretold, along with these words of hope: "Simon, Simon, behold, Satan has demanded permission to sift you like wheat; but I have prayed for you, that your faith may not fail; and you, when once you have turned again, strengthen your brothers" (Luke 22:31–32).

Peter was cocky, impatient, and impulsive before the cross and before his denial of our Lord. Having failed miserably but yet receiving the grace of God, Peter was restored. It was then that Peter's ministry truly began. There is a sense in which God uses our sin to instruct us and others as well. But he never causes us to sin, nor does he want us to. James 1:13–14 says, "Let no man say when he is tempted, I am tempted of God: for God cannot be tempted with evil, neither tempteth he any man: But every man is tempted, when he is drawn away of his own lust, and enticed."

This instruction may be as others observe the painful outcome of our sin (Prov. 19:25) or by observing the restoration and deepened sense of God's grace that is produced in the life of a repentant and restored sinner.

The Reward of Repentance

The fruit of David's divinely wrought repentance! God responded to David's repentance with grace, and thus, David responded graciously to those who wronged him and repented. When Absalom rebelled against his father and was about to take over the kingdom, David fled from Jerusalem with those who followed him. As he was leaving the city, a man named Shimei came out to curse David and to throw stones at him (2 Sam. 16:5–8). Abishai wanted to cut off his head, but David would not allow him to do so. When David returned to Jerusalem, one of those there to meet and welcome him was Shimei, who confessed to David that he had sinned in what he had done earlier (2 Sam. 19:16–20).

Abishai once again wanted to execute Shimei, and this time he had a biblical reason. He called attention to the fact that Shimei had cursed David, the king of Israel. The Law of Moses forbade cursing a ruler of the people (Exod. 22:28). Technically—or should I say "legally"—Shimei should have been put to death, but David forgave him and granted him his life. In so doing, David dealt with Shimei in the same gracious manner God had dealt with him.

This incident reminds us of the story our Lord told about the unforgiving slave (see Matthew 18:23–35), whose great debt had been forgiven by the king but who refused to forgive the smaller debt of his fellow slave. Those who have truly experienced God's grace manifest this same grace toward others. The grace David received as a result of his repentance he showed to a repentant Shimei.

David's repentance was real, and he did not repeat the sin. There are those like Pharaoh and Saul, who seem to repent, but their repentance is not real and short-lived. It certainly did not take Saul long to take up his efforts to kill David or Pharaoh to again resist Israel's departure from Egypt. This was because their repentance was not sincere. Their repentance was simply the path of least resistance and the way to temporarily stop the pain.

Stuart Briscoe differentiates between false repentance and real repentance. He said, "I remember a friend of mine in England who said something to me long ago. 'Baby repentance is *sorry* for what it has done. Adult repentance is *regretful* for what it is. If I am only sorry for what I have done, I am likely to go out and do it again." But regret is another story. Regret is a feeling of sadness, repentance, and disappointment over an event of the past. David manifested adult or real repentance. He saw his sin for what it was and was genuinely regretful. As a result, he did not repeat the awful sin of Uriah's situation. (See 2 Sam. 11.)

Conditions of Forgiveness

> And Nathan said to David, the LORD also has taken away your sin; you shall not die. (2 Sam. 12:13b)

What David did not dare to ask for, he received. What a wave of relief to hear those words from Nathan: "The LORD also has taken away your sin; you shall not die." David had condemned himself in his response to Nathan's story of the stolen and slaughtered pet lamb (2 Sam. 12:1–4). The Bible says, "Then David's anger burned greatly against the evil man of the story. He said to Nathan, 'As the LORD lives, surely the man who has done this deserves to die'" (2 Sam. 12:5).

Legally, of course, the Law of Moses would only have required fourfold restitution from the culprit of Nathan's story (Exod. 22:1). But David should have died, both for his adultery and for the murder of Uriah. Under the Law of Moses, David had no hope. He was a condemned man. He was a dead man!

How then is it possible for Nathan to tell David that he will not die? You will notice the promise that David will not die follows this statement:

"The Lord also has taken away your sin." David's salvation from divine condemnation, like ours, did not come from law-keeping, but by grace. And the reason David's sin could be forgiven was because the Lord had taken it away.

This "taking away" of sin is not some magic trick where God simply takes the sin of David and makes it disappear. It has been "taken away." I believe Nathan's statement can only have been made on the basis of the sure and certain work of Jesus Christ on the cross of Calvary, centuries later. On the basis of the work of Christ on Calvary, David is forgiven. His sins were borne by our Lord, and thus, God's justice was satisfied.

The expression "has taken away" in verse 13 of the NASB would literally render, "caused your sin to pass away." It is a common verb, often used with the sense of passing through or passing over, such as when the Israelites passed through the Red Sea so that the rendering, "caused to pass over or away," is found.

Both the New King James Version and the original King James Version render it "put away." I believe the Hebrew word found in our text is twice employed elsewhere in the Bible in a way that closely approximates the sense of the term in our text. Observe the following:

> Then Abner was very angry over the words of Ish-bosheth and said, "Am I a dog's head that belongs to Judah? Today I show kindness to the house of Saul your father, to his brothers and to his friends, and have not delivered you into the hands of David; and yet today you charge me with a guilt concerning the woman. May God do so to Abner, and more also, if as the Lord has sworn to David, I do not accomplish this for him, to transfer the kingdom from the house of Saul and to establish the throne of David over Israel and over Judah, from Dan even to Beersheba." (2 Sam. 3:8–10)

> The king took off his signet ring which he had taken away from Haman, and gave it to Mordecai. And Esther set Mordecai over the house of Haman" (Esther 8:2).

In both cases above, the same Hebrew term we find in our text is used to describe the "transfer" of something from one person to another. The kingdom of Israel was transferred from Saul to David (2 Sam. 3:8–10). The king's ring, giving a subordinate the authority to act on the king's behalf, was taken from Haman and given to Mordecai. The ring was transferred from one person to another.

David's sin was forgiven, and he was assured he would not die because God had transferred his sins. This transfer took place centuries later when David's "son," the Lord Jesus Christ, died on the cross of Calvary. David's sins were borne by our Lord, and He paid the penalty for what David had done. David would not die for his sin because Christ was destined to die, bearing the penalty for them.

Nathan speaks of this transfer as though it was a past event. Old Testament prophets often used the past tense to speak of a future event. They did this, it would seem, to emphasize the certainty of the prophesied event. When God promises to do something, it is as we say, "as good as done." When the prophet's spoke of God's future promises, they often did so by employing the past tense. Even centuries before the birth and death of Christ, men were granted forgiveness, based upon this event. David was forgiven because Christ died for his sins on the cross of Calvary.

This is the only basis for forgiveness. David rightly confessed that he had sinned against God, and now Nathan assures David that his sin against God has been forgiven by God, through the sacrificial and substitutionary death of the Son of God, Jesus Christ. This has always been the only basis for the forgiveness of sins.

7

Four Specific Steps to Seeing Yourself

Step 1: Get Closer to God! Get Close to His Word

Then Saul, still breathing threats and murder against the disciples of the Lord, went to the high priest and asked letters from him to the synagogues of Damascus, so that if he found any who were of the Way, whether men or women, he might bring them bound to Jerusalem. As he journeyed he came near Damascus, and suddenly a light shone around him from heaven.

Then he fell to the ground, and heard a voice saying to him, "Saul, Saul, why are you persecuting me?" And he said, "Who are You, Lord?" Then the Lord said, "I am Jesus, whom you are persecuting. It *is* hard for you to kick against the goads." So he, trembling and astonished, said, "Lord, what do you want me to do?" Then the Lord *said* to him, "Arise and go into the city, and you will be told what you must do." (Acts 9:1–7, KJV)

A glimpse of God through the text, hopefully, has brought you to a better understanding of who you are. This kindling of the word should light your fire to be better and the oil of knowing Jesus should keep the fire burning. Acknowledge that Saul, before contact with Jesus, thought he was doing "good" and "right." You may acknowledge similar relations. You were active in your day-to-day routine of living (giving alms, visiting the sick, serving on the boards, and the like) but really were fighting against the work of the kingdom, instead of supporting it.

Also, like Saul, if asked about your activity, you would not acknowledge your opposition to the principles of God, either because you simply and honestly have not thought about it or just don't realize your position opposes God. Yet the reality is, you were a hindrance and not a help. Though unlike Paul who publicly participated in the stoning of Stephen, you threw your rocks and hid your hands privately. You initiated the plot, gossip, or evil thought but had another carry it out. To see yourself and to become better, you need remove all obstacles by repenting and thus clearing the pathway to God. You can do it right now. Ask God to forgive you before it's everlastingly too late. We will wait for you, okay?

Hopefully, like Saul, you will receive a word from the Lord on your Damascus Road of life and become a Paul. It needs noting that Jesus plans assignments for those who both recognize his voice and to those who are stubborn, for those who walk the path of discipleship faithfully, and for those who resolutely walk the other way. Saul was both an enemy of God and Christ and actively working against them, though he would have denied he was opposing God. Saul did not know Christ, but he thought he was working for God as he disposed of this Christian sect of heretics.

Acts 8:1–3 reflects this:

> Now Saul was consenting to his death. At that time a great persecution arose against the church which was at Jerusalem; and they were all scattered throughout the regions of Judea and Samaria, except the apostles. And devout men carried Stephen to his burial, and made great lamentation over him. As for Saul, he made havoc of the church, entering every house, and dragging off men and women, committing them to prison.

But whether acknowledged or not, the words of Jesus clarifies that "He that is not with me is against me; and he that gathereth not with me, scattereth abroad (Matt. 12:30). Yet when God called Saul's name for service, he responded, "Who are thou, Lord?" This reminds those that think one has to have his/her act altogether before Jesus will call you for participation, think again. Sometimes it takes Jesus (through revelation, inspiration, or the written Word) to let you know that you don't have your act together since you cannot see yourself. Yet most of the time, people are blind and won't listen to any body other than Jesus. There are times when even the husband, wife (and sometimes, especially the husband or wife), sibling, children, mother, and dad can't tell you anything.

But hopefully the Lord intervenes; and your life is turned upside down and nothing is ever the same again. At other times, he calls and even comes to you simply for a season. He just gives you time to do your task, and when it's over, you return to life as usual. Whichever the case, when God calls, he calls you out of your comfort zone. The record of history testifies to this truth. Hebrews 11 says,

By faith Noah warned about what was not yet seen, with reverence built an ark for the salvation of his household. Through this he condemned the world and inherited the righteousness that comes through faith. By faith Abraham obeyed when he was called to go out to a place that he was to receive as an inheritance; he went out, not knowing where he was to go. By faith he sojourned in the Promised Land as in a foreign country, dwelling in tents with Isaac and Jacob, heirs of the same promise; What more shall I say? I have not time to tell of Gideon, Barak, Samson, Jephthah, of David and Samuel and the prophets, who by faith conquered kingdoms, did what was righteous, obtained the promises; they closed the mouths of lions, put out raging fires, escaped the devouring sword; out of weakness they were made powerful, became strong in battle, and turned back foreign invaders. Women received back their dead through resurrection. Some were tortured and would not accept deliverance, in order to obtain a better resurrection. Others endured mockery, scourging, even chains and imprisonment. They were stoned, sawed in two, put to death at sword's point; they went about in skins of sheep or goats, needy, afflicted, tormented. The world was not worthy of them. They wandered about in deserts and on mountains, in caves and in crevices in the earth. Yet all these, though approved because of their faith, did not receive what had been promised. God had foreseen something better for us, so that without us they should not be made perfect. (Heb. 11:7–40)

Like you, myself, and many others in history, Saul was focused on a purpose of his own. He never expected to encounter the Lord Jesus on the road to Damascus. He never expected to have his life turned upside-down. He never expected to become an evangelist for Jesus Christ. But the Lord called, and nothing was ever the same again.

Ananias was understandably concerned about the suggestion of going to see Saul. It didn't make sense to him and involved taking a considerable risk. But the Lord called, so he responded. For one brief moment, he stepped into the spotlight in response to God's call, and after which, stepped back into the background and went on with his life.

The Lord provided Saul with everything he needed to fulfill his assignment. The Lord provided Ananias with everything he needed to fulfill his assignment. The Lord provides you and me with everything we need to fulfill our assignments. As Abraham discovered, the Lord provides. He is Jehovah-Jireh.

Additionally, many times when the Lord calls, he has to do some changing in you before you can go out and change the world. Therefore, it is imperative that we see and accept the change God is dictating. When Saul lost his sight for three days, more was going on than just a physical reaction to a bright light. Somewhere in the wilderness, alone with God, the Lord was letting Saul know how blind he was; and that his rejection of Jesus was the result of that blindness. His zealousness in persecuting the church was also the result of blindness, even his devotion to the Law was blind devotion. Again note; Saul was blind in one and could not see out of the other.

When Ananias laid his hands upon Saul and the scales fell from his eyes, more was going on than a physical healing of damaged eyes. It was a signal to Saul of the many dramatic changes that would take place. One such example is when Paul and his companions passed through Amphipolis and Apollonia, they came to Thessalonica, where there was a Jewish synagogue. As was his custom, Paul went into the synagogue, and on three Sabbath days he reasoned with them from the Scriptures, explaining and proving that the Messiah had to suffer and rise from the dead (Acts 17:1).

Step 2: Overcoming Selfishness

Earlier in the introduction, the book disclosed the characteristics of selfishness. This chapter will disclose the secrets to overcoming it. Notice first that the Scripture says, "Then said Jesus unto his disciples, If any man will come after me, let him deny himself, and take up his cross and follow me" (Matt. 16:24).

There are many descriptive remedies in the Bible to overcoming selfishness. As stated above within the Synoptic gospels and noting Mark

8:27 particularly, Jesus conducted his public ministry. He spoke to large crowds and taught them about the kingdom of God, and his performance of miracles proved his authority. He paused again to ask the disciples to make a commitment. He said, "Who do you think that I the Son of man is? Peter, speaking for the twelve says, "We believe you are the Christ, the Messiah, God's king who was to come into the world."

Notice that Jesus accepts Peter's confession as true. But observe what happens next, everything changes. Much of Jesus's ministry became private. He did not perform as many miracles as before and primarily taught the twelve disciples about the rules and regulations of God's kingdom.

Then in verse 34, Jesus goes straight to the heart of the gospel. He says, "If anyone would come after me, let him deny himself and take up his cross and follow me." If anyone (man or woman, boy or girl) wants to follow Jesus, to be his disciple and become a Christian, he/she must do at least three things. They must "deny themselves, take up their cross, and follow Jesus." Luke inserts and clarifies Jesus's directives. He says we are to take up our cross "daily" (Luke 9:23). What does this mean? Christians must overcome selfishness (defined as putting self over everything else daily).

Barriers to Overcome Selfishness

- **Psychological breakdown of the id, ego, etc.**

    Jesus says that the first step is possessing a relationship with God. This is necessary for many reasons.

    First: God's spirit is needed to assist you to make the necessary changes, changes from pride to humility. The ability to accept facts of reality. Going from disbelief to belief and understanding that none are better than others and each man is his brother's keeper, etc. Second: There is a need to understand the obstacles; love is one.

- **Love is not only blind, but it blinds.**

    Love is an intoxicant, like drugs and alcohol. The commercial says, "Don't trust your judgment when drinking alcohol. Don't trust your judgment when in love. You are not at your best decision-making stage.

An article from youramazingbrain.org/lovesex/sciencelove states the following:

Helen Fisher of Rutgers University in the States has proposed 3 stages of love—lust, attraction and attachment. Each stage is driven by different hormones and chemicals.

Stage 1: Lust

This is the first stage of love and is driven by the sex hormones testosterone and oestrogen—in both men and women.

Stage 2: Attraction

This is the amazing time when you are truly love-struck and can think of little else. Scientists think that three main neuro-transmitters are involved in this stage; adrenaline, dopamine and serotonin.

Adrenaline

The initial stages of falling for someone activates your stress response, increasing your blood levels of adrenalin and cortisol. This has the charming effect that when you unexpectedly bump into your new love, you start to sweat, your heart races and your mouth goes dry.

Dopamine

Helen Fisher asked newly 'love struck' couples to have their brains examined and discovered they have high levels of the neurotransmitter dopamine. This chemical stimulates 'desire and reward' by triggering an intense rush of pleasure. It has the same effect on the brain as taking cocaine!

Fisher suggests "couples often show the signs of surging dopamine: increased energy, less need for sleep or food, focused attention and exquisite delight in smallest details of this novel relationship."

Serotonin

And finally, serotonin. One of love's most important chemicals that may explain why when you're falling in love, your new lover keeps popping into your thoughts.

Does love change the way you think?

A landmark experiment in Pisa, Italy showed that early love (the attraction phase) really changes the way you think.

Dr. Donatella Marazziti, a psychiatrist at the University of Pisa advertised for twenty couples who'd been madly in love for less than six months. She wanted to see if the brain mechanisms that cause you to constantly think about your lover, were related to the brain mechanisms of Obsessive-Compulsive Disorder.

By analyzing blood samples from people in love, Dr. Marazitti discovered that serotonin levels of newly found lovers were equivalent to the low serotonin levels of Obsessive-Compulsive Disorder patients. Beware of love, it triggers obsessive compulsive emotions.

Love Not only is blind, but blinds!

Newly smitten lovers often idealize their partner, magnifying their virtues and explaining away their flaws says Ellen Berscheid, a leading researcher on the psychology of love.

Love causes new couples to exalt the relationship blindly. "It's very common to think they have a relationship that's closer and more special than anyone else's." Psychologists think we need this rose-tinted view. This initial phase makes people want to stay together in order to enter the next stage of love—attachment.

Stage 3: Attachment

Attachment is the bond that keeps couples together long enough for them to have and raise children. Scientists think there might be two major hormones involved in this feeling of attachment; oxytocin and vasopressin.

Oxytocin—The cuddle hormone:

Oxytocin is a powerful hormone released by men and women during the love experience.

It probably deepens the feelings of attachment and makes couples feel much closer to one another after the love experience. The theory goes that the more love experiences a couple has, the deeper their bond becomes.

Oxytocin also seems to help cement the strong bond between mothers and babies and is released during childbirth. It is also responsible for a mother's breast automatically releasing milk at the mere sight or sound of her young baby.

Diane Witt, assistant professor of psychology from New York has showed that if you block the natural release of oxytocin in sheep and rats, they reject their own young.

Conversely, injecting oxytocin into female rats who've never had a love experience (sex), caused them to fawn over another female's young, nuzzling the pups and protecting them as if they were their own.

Vasopressin

Vasopressin is another important hormone in the long-term commitment stage and is released after Romantic involvement.

Vasopressin (also called anti-diuretic hormone) works with your kidneys to control thirst. Its potential role in long-term relationships was discovered when scientists looked at the prairie vole. Prairie voles indulge in far more sex than is strictly necessary for the purposes of reproduction. They also—like humans—form fairly stable pair-bonds.

When male prairie voles were given a drug that suppresses the effect of vasopressin, the bond with their partner deteriorated immediately as they lost their devotion and failed to protect their partner from new suitors.

Take note of the steps to falling in love NO ch

Be careful when dealing with strangers.

Don't reveal to each other intimate details about your lives.

Don't dare stare deeply into each other's eyes without talking.

As seen by the physical and psychological evidence, Love Blinds, but also does Hate!

According to News Science (article), scientists prove it really is a thin line between love and hate. The same brain circuitry is involved in both extreme emotions; but hate retains a semblance of rationality. Scientists studying the physical nature of hate have found that some of the nervous circuits in the brain responsible for it are the same as those that are used during the feeling of romantic love—although love and hate appear to be polar opposites. A study using a brain scanner to investigate the neural circuits that become active when people look at a photograph of someone they say they hate has found that the "hate circuit" shares something in common with the love circuit. The findings could explain why both hate and romantic love can result in similar acts of extreme behavior—both heroic and evil— said Professor Semir Zeki of University College London, who led the study published in the on-line journal PloS ONE.

"Hate is also often considered to be an evil passion that should, in a better world, be tamed, controlled and eradicated. Yet to the biologist, hate is a passion that is of equal interest to love," Professor Zeki said. "Like love, it is often seemingly irrational and can lead individual to heroic and evil deeds. How can two opposite sentiments lead to the same behavior?"

One major difference between love and hate appears to be in the fact that large parts of the cerebral cortex—associated with judgement and reasoning—become de-activated during love, whereas only a small area is deactivated in hate.

"This may seem surprising since hate can also be an all-consuming passion like love. But whereas in romantic love, the lover is often less critical and judgmental regarding the loved person, it is more likely that in the context of hate the hater may want to exercise judgment in calculating moves to harm, injure or otherwise exact revenge," Professor Zeki said. (http://www.independent.co.uk/news/science/scientists-prove-it-really-is-a-thin-line-between-love-and-hate-976901.html)

Thus, one must acknowledge hatred as well as love because it diminishes the capacity to make wise decisions. So the same recommendations used to assist people in love are recommended in hatred as well. Again, News Science says, "Hate, as a mode of guilt or of pride, generates destructive thoughts (but at a lesser intensity than paranoia). Antithetical thoughts, when directed to other people, represent pride; when directed to oneself, represent guilt. [1]. At a much lesser intensity of denigration, criticisms of other people represent jealousy, whilst criticisms of ourselves arise from senses of idealism."

As love not only is blind, but it also blinds! Hatred does the same. Before acting in hatred, follow these steps:

1. Study the word of God for direction.

    We love because God first loved us. Whoever says, "I love God," but hates his brother is a liar. The one who does not love his brother whom he has seen cannot love the God whom he has not seen. (1 John 4:19–20)

    Again, a new commandment I write unto you, which thing is true in him and in you: because the darkness is past, and the true light now shineth. He that saith he is in the light, and hateth his brother, is in darkness even until now. He that loveth his brother abideth in the light, and there is none occasion of stumbling in him. But he that hateth his brother is in darkness, and walketh in darkness, and knoweth not whither he goeth, because that darkness hath blinded his eyes. (1 John 2:8–11)

2. Seek a parent's advice.
3. Seek a friend's advice.
4. Seek professional help from a pastor, psychologist, counselor, etc.

Step 3: There Are Times to Take Your Own Advice; and Times Not To

Fools think their own way is right, but the wise listen to others. (Prov. 12:15)

It's not easy taking your own advice, accepting what you don't like hearing, and seeing the gray amongst the black and white. But do what you tell your children to do when your circumstances are the same as theirs. If it was right for them, it's right for you. Don't make excuses for you not doing what you know is right and what you tell others to do.

Giving advice is pretty easy. Anyone can give advice. Anyone can make recommendations. Anyone can tell others what to do, especially when it comes to friends and acquaintances. People are always trying to find ways to help others out. Most friends look out for each other, and when someone close is going through a rough time with a job, mate, finances, etc., the natural response is to try and help them figure out what to do about it. Many spend hours and even weeks at a time giving best friends advice. We say, "Don't sleep with them," "Don't smoke that," "Don't go there," "Be careful," "Don't get hurt," etc. We're so careful giving advice. We treat their lives like newborn babies—fragile and in need of delicate care. We care so much about other's lives, yet we are even more reckless with our own.

On many occasions, most people's own lives are a wreck. She slept with a different him, smoked a different that, went there and shouldn't have, was careless instead of cautious, and got hurt. Your friends gave you the same advice you earlier gave them, but you didn't listen. People give out all this sage advice but rarely take it themselves. Personally, we expect our friends to value our advice, but we ignore this same advice in regards to our own problems.

Do we think we're not worth the advice? Or do we simply think we don't need it? We are worthy, and we do need it. Sure, we're adults who can make our own decisions, but sometimes we need a fresh perspective on things, the same kind of fresh perspective we're trying to give our friends when we hand out advice. When we look at our own life, it's just as messy as the lives of our friends who we're trying to help. Why do they need cleaning up but we can live through the mess? We need to learn to take our own advice or stop giving it. Why waste our breath if we wouldn't do the things we're saying ourselves? We can't be so hypocritical. If you tell your friend not to do something that you would probably do, what's the point?

Sometimes we act all high and mighty with our friends, as if we know what they should be doing with their time and decisions. Even if we had our life together, we wouldn't have the right to do that, and what's worse is that we don't really have anything together. The same decisions they're struggling with, we struggle with too. None of us know. How do we help each other then? That fresh perspective we're always trying to give each other? We need to keep giving it, but we need to be regifting it from our friends to ourselves.

When a friend is stuck and doesn't know what to do about something, we start brainstorming solutions we can throw at them. The next time your best friend is trying to decide what to do about that guy that isn't treating her right, as you dole out your advice, think to yourself, "Have I ever needed to hear this advice myself?" We often justify to ourselves why our problems are so much different. "Oh no," we think, "her man treats her much worse than mine does, even though he never texts me back. But still, it's different."

No, it's not different. Listen to the advice you're giving your friend. If she doesn't take it, that's fine. You came up with it, and there is no excuse. But when it's your turn, take your own advice. It's natural to want to help and give advice to our friends. Sometimes we actually do know more on a subject than they do, and so our guidance is well-justified. On many occasions though, they're dealing with the same crazy young twenty-something mess we are. When giving advice, we need to start recognizing that this is something we need to try too. It might even feel more collaborative if two friends together decide we're going to take the advice we give each other and actually try to make a change. If we start remembering this more often, to take our own advice, we might start being a little less messy ourselves. Maybe. If not, no worries. There's a lot of advice to go around and a lot of years left to hear it in.

It's often easy to give advice to other people when they are having relationship trouble. It's typical for a friend to ask a friend for advice. Having a conflict with a coworker? We ask another coworker for advice. Having money problems? We seek advice, etc. You get the idea. Sometimes, all we have to do is look in the mirror and ask ourselves for advice. Who knows you better than you? Nobody is more aware of your situation. Nobody is more familiar with every scenario and potential outcome. Just because someone spouts their opinion, though, doesn't mean it's the correct advice for you.

So why do we turn to others so often? Because it's easy. If someone tells us what to do, we don't have to think. Coincidentally—or not so coincidentally—this is also how fascism works: someone else makes the decisions for you. Or sometimes we ask other people for advice to reaffirm our own, but other people rarely have the same stake in the outcome, which makes their opinion less valid than ours. It's okay to ask others for advice; sometimes it's great to have a fresh pair of eyes and a new set of ears. But remember that it is you who must live with your decisions. To help you make wise decisions, here's some words of wisdom from the wise old folks of the past.

- A bird in the hand is worth two in the bush.—Latin proverb
- A good example is the best sermon.—English (on advice)
- A penny saved is a penny earned.—Scottish proverb
- A stitch in time saves nine.—unknown
- Advice after mischief is like medicine after death.—Danish (on advice)
- Advise no one to go to war or marry.—Spanish (on advice)
- Avoid a cure that is worse than the disease.—Aesop (c. 620 BC–560 BC)
- Before you marry keep, both eyes open; after marriage, keep one eye shut.—Jamaican
- Better late than never.—Roman proverb

- Better three hours too soon than a minute too late.—William Shakespeare (1564–1616)
- Choose the hills wisely on which you must do battle.—unknown
- Do "good" to thy friend to keep him, to thy enemy to gain him.—Ben Franklin (1706–1790)
- Don't believe everything you hear.—Aesop (c. 620 BC–560 BC)
- Early to bed and early to rise makes a man healthy, wealthy, and wise.—Ben Franklin
- Focus on what's right in your world instead of what's wrong.—unknown
- Get out of harm's way.—Miguel de Cervantes (1547–1616)
- Grin and bear it.—unknown
- If you are hiding, don't light a fire.—Ghanaian (on common sense)
- If you can't bite, better not show your teeth.—Yiddish (on common sense)
- Interest on debt grows without rain.—Yiddish (on indebtedness)
- It is better to prevent than to cure.—Peruvian (on common sense)
- It is easy to advise the wise.—Serbian (on advice)
- Keep an open mind.—unknown
- Lend your money and lose your friend.—William Caxton (1421–1491)
- Live life to the fullest because you may not have it tomorrow.—reader's name lost
- Live your own life for you will die your own death.—Latin (on life and living)
- Make haste slowly.—Suetonius (c. 69 AD–140 AD)
- Marry in haste, repent in leisure.—unknown
- Neither a borrower nor a lender be.—William Shakespeare (1564–1616)
- Never give advice unasked.—unknown

- Never spend your money before you make it.—unknown
- One day at a time.—unknown
- Out of debt, out of danger.—unknown
- Put on your thinking cap.—unknown
- Rather go to bed supper-less than run in debt for a breakfast.—Ben Franklin (1706–1790)
- Save for a rainy day.—Aesop (c. 620 BC–560 BC)
- Seek advice but use your own common sense.—Yiddish (on advice)
- Seize the day.—unknown
- Spending is quick; earning is slow.

Step 4: Do Unto Others

The premier part played by the Golden Rule

> So whatever you wish that others would do to you, do also to them, for this is the Law and the Prophets. (Matt. 7:12, ESV)

> The second is this: "You shall love your neighbor as yourself." There is no other commandment greater than these. (Mark 12:31, ESV)

> If anyone says, "I love God," and hates his brother, he is a liar; for he who does not love his brother whom he has seen cannot love God whom he has not seen. (1 John 4:20, ESV)

The Golden Rule or ethic of reciprocity is a maxim, ethical code, or morality that essentially states either of the following:

> Positive form of Golden Rule: One should treat others as one would like others to treat oneself.
>   Negative form of Golden Rule: One should not treat others in ways that one would not like to be treated (also known as the Silver Rule.)

This concept describes a reciprocal or two-way relationship between oneself and others. It involves both sides equally and in a mutual fashion.

The Golden Rule concept can be explained from the perspective of psychology, philosophy, sociology, and religion. Psychologically, it involves a person empathizing with others. Philosophically, it involves a person perceiving their neighbor as "I" or "self." Sociologically, it is applicable between individuals, between groups, and between individuals and groups. (For example, a person living by this rule treats all people with consideration, not just members of his or her in-group).

> Religion is an integral part of the history of this concept. As a *concept*, the Golden Rule has a history that long predates the *term* "Golden Rule," or "Golden law," as it was called from the 1670s. As a concept of "the ethic of reciprocity," it has its roots in a wide range of world cultures. It is a standard way that different cultures use to resolve conflicts. It has a long history, and a great number of prominent religious figures and philosophers have restated its reciprocal, "two-way" nature. (Wikipedia, the free encyclopedia)

The Golden Rule is another measure to help you see yourself and be the best you can be in order to be blessed by God. I am sure you have shopped at J. C. Penney at some time or other, but here's something that you probably did not know about Penney's. It used to be known as "the Golden Rule store." In fact, in 1898, Penney began working for a small chain of stores in the western United States called the Golden Rule stores. In 1902, owners Guy Johnson and Thomas Callahan, impressed by his work ethic and salesmanship, offered him one-third partnership in a new store he would open. Penney invested two thousand dollars and moved to Kemmerer, Wyoming, to open a store there called the "Golden Rule store."

Another thing, you probably did not know about Mr. J. C. Penney. He did not like to refer to those that worked for him as "employees." Instead, he called his employees "associates." This is another concept given to man from Jesus. John 15:15 says, "Henceforth I call you not servants; for the servant knoweth not what his lord doeth: but I have called you friends; for all things that I have heard of my Father I have made known unto you." He treated them just like he wanted to be treated. He took a general store in 1902 and turned it into a multibillion-dollar business because he actually lived the Golden Rule. He treated employees with love, respect, kindness, understanding, and encouragement.

Do you try to treat others in your life like this? The normal instinct is to be nice to people who are nice to us. But that's not what Jesus taught. Jesus did not say, "Treat people with the same respect, love, kindness, consideration, forgiveness, etc. that they treat you with." He said, "Whatever you want men and women to do to you, do to them."

To do that, love is the key. Remember, that is why Christian maturity begins with placing Jesus Christ at the center of our hearts. It is only through Him that we find love enough to love people as we love ourselves.

Matthew 5:43–44 informs us, "You have heard it said, 'Love your neighbor and hate your enemy.' I tell you, 'Love your enemy and pray for those who persecute you.'" Mankind is commanded to love everyone. That is how Jesus lived on this earth, and if we are Christians, we must strive to be like Christ. How will the world know that we are Christians if we do not love one another?

They will not know that by reading a sign on our foreheads or one over our doors. They will only know, by the love we have in our hearts for other people. Andrew Murray said, "My relationship with God is part of my relationship with men. Failure in one will cause failure in the other."

John Ashcroft said, "The most important thing my dad taught me is that there are more important things than me." There is an old saying that goes like this: "A pat on the back is only a few vertebrae away from a kick in the butt, but the results are much better."

Look at yourself

1. Has your attitude been golden lately?

    Have you been able to demonstrate the Golden or Silver Rule in your attitude lately? Many people will say they can do that with ease "if only"….

    …they measure up to my standards.

    ….they do things my way.

    If only, if only, if only!

    Jesus did not say "if and when only" they do something for you first. He commanded us to love people, even when they didn't meet any of our high and mighty criteria.

    There was a man once sitting by a tree near a creek, reading his Bible. Something caught his eye, and he looked to see a scorpion caught between two roots of the tree. The man reached over to help the scorpion loose, but each time he tried to grab it, the scorpion tried to sting him. A man who was standing nearby watching this said, "Don't you know it is the scorpion's nature to sting? Why don't you just forget it and let it die there?"

The man smiled and looked up and replied, "Should it be necessary that I change my nature to accommodate someone else's nature? The scorpion's nature may be to sting, but my nature is to love and help." When God's love fills your heart, you cannot help but share it and with all people and things.

Jesus observed two ways of giving. One way is to give, in hopes that you will get something out of it. That is like the man who bought his wife a ping-pong table for her birthday. He knew she wanted it, but he expected to use it as much as she did. In effect, he didn't just give to her; he gave to himself with the expectation of using it more than her. When we give with expectations of receiving, that's really not giving.

The only way to give like God gave is without any expectation of getting anything back. This is the example of Christ. The best way to show your love is through free giving. You give simply because you want others to be fulfilled, and you sacrifice your feelings for someone else's feelings. What you feel on the inside of your heart determines what you demonstrate on the outside with your attitude. Philippians 2:5 says, "Let this mind be in you, which was also in Christ Jesus." In other words, your attitude should be the same as Jesus. How has your attitude been toward others? Has it been golden?

2. Do you have an attitude of success?

Jesus made a statement that is perhaps the most important key to success that you will ever encounter. It is so basic that even a child can understand it, yet it is so profound that none of us can live up to it without the power of Jesus.

What is the statement that Jesus made? It is the one that most of us learned as children. It is in Matthew 7:12: "So in everything, do to others what you would have them do to you, for this sum's up the law and the Prophets."

Jesus's whole ministry was seeking the blessings of God and doing his will. But right in the middle of it, He seems to have thrown us a curve ball. Now, not only do we have to live in right standing with Him but we also have to live in right standing with other people. He basically told us that if we treat others as good as we want to be treated, we will receive God's blessings for doing that. We are evaluated by God and rewarded in direct proportion to the way we treat and feel about other people. That is scary, isn't it? But to be successful as Christians, we must do this.

There is a story of a young boy who had been invited to attend a friend's birthday party and was eagerly awaiting the day he could go. On that day, however, there was a near blizzard outside, and his father thought it was too dangerous for him to walk the short three blocks to his friend's house and that it was much too dangerous to drive the boy.

The little boy reacted tearfully and begged his father to let him go. Finally, the father recanted and gave his permission. The boy bundled himself up started walking down the street. The wind and snow blew so hard against him that what should have only taken ten minutes took nearly an hour.

Finally, the boy got to the house. As he rang the doorbell, he looked back to see the shadowy figure of his father disappearing into the snow. His father had followed every footstep to make sure the boy was safe.

It is all about sacrifice, isn't it? When we are able to sacrifice what we want, what we need, and what we think so that we can freely give to someone else what they want or need, we have proven ourselves successful as a Christian.

Has your attitude been one of success in Christ lately?

3. How do you normally treat others?

A brother and sister were in the attic looking through love letters their parents had written to each other many years ago. The boy asked, "Are you sure these belong to Mom and Dad?" The sister assured him that they did. He then told her, "That's not the names they call each other now!"

Did you know that each time you talk negatively to your spouse, you are actually robbing him or her of some of their self-worth? Yet how many times do we come home very tired or get busy concentrating on something just to snap at the other?

In those situations, we would never think about saying that we didn't love them, so why are we talking to them in such a way that our actions says it to them?

The marriage counselor told the husband to start being more attentive to the wife and start treating her with more love. So one day he comes home a little early with a dozen roses in one hand and a box of chocolates in the other. His wife opens the door, sees him, and angrily burst into tears. In between sobs, she says, "Little Johnny threw up, your parents called and said they were coming over for dinner, and to top it all off, you come home drunk!" (She thought he had to be drunk to bring flowers. Did you get it?)

This describes too many people today. There are too many families so torn apart they don't know how to accept change, even when it is for the good. In Philippians 2:4–5, we are told how our attitudes are supposed to be. "Each of you should look not only to your own interests, but also to the interest of others. Your attitude should be the same as that of Christ Jesus."

Think about this: a farmer must sow his seeds before he is able to reap a crop. Likewise, we must sow our seeds before we can reap our crops. The difference is the seed a farmer uses might be corn or wheat. The seeds we sow are the seeds of love from our hearts, and the crop we reap are the rewards of God's love for us. Galatians 6:7 reminds us, "Do not be deceived, God is not mocked; for whatever a man sows, that he will also reap."

It is a process that begins in our thoughts. What we think about becomes our primary focus. Our primary focus will soon seep into our words and very quickly, our words reinforce that focus into our actions. There is a quicker way of saying it: "Garbage in, garbage out." And, it works every single time. Someone once said, "If you will cheat in practice, you will cheat in the game. If you cheat other people, you will cheat God. And when you cheat God, you cheat yourself." Another person said, "Sow a thought, reap an act. Sow an act, reap a habit. Sow a habit, reap a character.

Sow a character, reap your eternity." The farmer cannot expect to reap a crop of corn if he plants the seed of wheat. You reap what you sow. What have you sowed lately?

Little Chad was in second grade. He was a little slower than the other children and that made them shun Chad. A couple of weeks before Valentine's Day, Chad came home and told his mother that he wanted to make cards for everyone in his class. She knew how they treated her son, but she helped him make thirty-five cards.

On Valentine's Day, she waited by the curb for the school bus to bring him home. When it got there, she saw all the kids laughing and getting off the bus, and then she saw Chad walking by himself near the back of the bus. When he got off the bus, he was very happy, and he told his mother that he didn't forget a single classmate and that he remembered them all. They still shunned Chad, but he remembered each one of them with a card.

Many have shunned Jesus Christ from the very beginning too, but he remembers each one with His love. He wants us to show that love to other people too, just like Chad did—for the sake of loving and not for the purpose of receiving anything back.

Obedience is not always easy. His classmates were not treating that little boy very well. But he treated them the way he wanted to be treated, not the way he was being treated. That little boy was living the Golden Rule. Can you say the same thing?

If this lost and hurting world is going to come to the saving knowledge of Jesus Christ, it will not be from some epiphany of sorts. It will be from people like you and me showing the love of Christ to others from our hearts.

We must be careful because there is a lie sweeping our nation that says, "I accepted Jesus years ago and was baptized, so I know I am saved today." If you forsake the Lord altogether and turn back to the world, the question becomes, Did you really get saved? It takes more than talk; it takes a walk with the Lord daily. Jesus said, And he said to them all, "If any man will come after me, let him deny himself, and take up his cross daily, and follow me (Luke 9:23, KJV). James says, "Faith without works is dead."

Let us be very careful with how we choose to believe lies. Let us be just as careful with the absolute knowledge that we are saved rather than just thinking we are.

Remember the man I mentioned earlier that tried to free that scorpion so it could live? Jesus came to earth in hopes of freeing us so that we might also live. If you need further proof of God's position, note the following:

The Biblical Commands to Do unto Others

So whatever you wish that others would do to you, do also to them, for this is the Law and the Prophets. (Matt. 7:12, ESV)

If anyone says, "I love God," and hates his brother, he is a liar; for he who does not love his brother whom he has seen cannot love God whom he has not seen. (1 John 4:20, ESV)

You shall not take vengeance or bear a grudge against the sons of your own people, but you shall love your neighbor as yourself: I am the Lord. (Lev. 19:18, ESV)

When the Son of Man comes in his glory, and all the angels with him, then he will sit on his glorious throne. Before him will be gathered all the nations, and he will separate people one from another as a shepherd separates the sheep from the goats. And he will place the sheep on his right, but the goats on the left. Then the King will say to those on his right, 'Come, you who are blessed by my Father, inherit the kingdom prepared for you from the foundation of the world. For I was hungry and you gave me food, I was thirsty and you gave me drink, I was a stranger and you welcomed me. (Matt. 25:31–46, ESV)

As for the one who is weak in faith, welcome him, but not to quarrel over opinions. (Rom. 14:1, ESV)

If you really fulfill the royal law according to the Scripture, "You shall love your neighbor as yourself," you are doing well. (James 2:8, ESV)

For if you forgive others their trespasses, your heavenly Father will also forgive you, but if you do not forgive others their trespasses, neither will your Father forgive your trespasses. (Matt. 6:14–15, ESV)

You have heard that it was said, "An eye for an eye and a tooth for a tooth." But I say to you, Do not resist the one who is evil. But if anyone slaps you on the right cheek, turn to him the other also. And if anyone would sue you and take your tunic, let him have your cloak as well. (Matt. 5:38–40, esv)

Brothers, if anyone is caught in any transgression, you who are spiritual should restore him in a spirit of gentleness. Keep watch on yourself, lest you too be tempted. Bear one another's burdens, and so fulfill the law of Christ. For if anyone thinks he is something, when he is nothing, he deceives himself. (Gal. 6:1–3, esv)

We who are strong have an obligation to bear with the failings of the weak, and not to please ourselves. Let each of us please his neighbor for his good, to build him up. (Rom. 15:1–2, esv)

Repay no one evil for evil, but give thought to do what is honorable in the sight of all. If possible, so far as it depends on you, live peaceably with all. Beloved, never avenge yourselves, but leave it to the wrath of God, for it is written, "Vengeance is mine, I will repay, says the Lord." To the contrary, "if your enemy is hungry, feed him; if he is thirsty, give him something to drink; for by so doing you will heap burning coals on his head." Do not be overcome by evil, but overcome evil with good. (Rom. 12:17–21, esv)

Therefore you have no excuse, O man, every one of you who judges. For in passing judgment on another you condemn yourself, because you, the judge, practice the very same things. We know that the judgment of God rightly falls on those who practice such things. Do you suppose, O man—you who judge those who practice such things and yet do them yourself—that you will escape the judgment of God? Or do you presume on the riches of his kindness and forbearance and patience, not knowing that God's kindness is meant to lead you to repentance? (Rom. 2:1–4, esv)

The woman said to him, "Sir, I perceive that you are a prophet. Our fathers worshiped on this mountain, but you say that in Jerusalem is the place where people ought to worship." Jesus said to her, "Woman, believe me, the hour is coming when neither on this mountain nor in Jerusalem will you worship the Father." (John 4:19–21, esv)

For God so loved the world, that he gave his only Son, that whoever believes in him should not perish but have eternal life. (John 3:16, esv)

Then Peter came up and said to him, "Lord, how often will my brother sin against me, and I forgive him? As many as seven times?" Jesus said to him, "I do not say to you seven times, but seventy times seven.

Therefore the kingdom of heaven may be compared to a king who wished to settle accounts with his servants. When he began to settle, one was brought to him who owed him ten thousand talents. And since he could not pay, his master ordered him to be sold, with his wife and children and all that he had, and payment to be made." (Matt. 18:21–35)

And as Jesus reclined at table in the house, behold, many tax collectors and sinners came and were reclining with Jesus and his disciples. And when the Pharisees saw this, they said to his disciples, "Why does your teacher eat with tax collectors and sinners?" But when he heard it, he said, "Those who are well have no need of a physician, but those who are sick. Go and learn what this means, 'I desire mercy, and not sacrifice.' For I came not to call the righteous, but sinners." (Matt. 9:10–13)

Not everyone who says to me, "Lord, Lord," will enter the kingdom of heaven, but the one who does the will of my Father who is in heaven. On that day many will say to me, "Lord, Lord, did we not prophesy in your name, and cast out demons in your name, and do many mighty works in your name?" And then will I declare to them, "I never knew you; depart from me, you workers of lawlessness." (Matt. 7:21–23)

Beware of practicing your righteousness before other people in order to be seen by them, for then you will have no reward from your Father who is in heaven. Thus, when you give to the needy, sound no trumpet before you, as the hypocrites do in the synagogues and in the streets, that they may be praised by others. Truly, I say to you they have received their reward. (Matt. 6:1–2)

The fact that humans can't see themselves as others see them has brought about complete chaos and devastation.

8

A Friend in Need Is a Friend Indeed

Knowing yourself the way you do, would you be your friend?

> I no longer call you servants, because a servant does not know his master's business. Instead, I have called you friends, for everything that I learned from my Father I have made known to you. You did not choose me, but I chose you and appointed you so that you might go and bear fruit—fruit that will last—and so that whatever you ask in my name the Father will give you. (John 15:15–16)

First consider the question "Would you be your friend?" when you honestly reminisce about how you treat your friends. As stated above, if you are not caring and sensitive to their situations, you are not a friend in the true sense of the word. I almost said, you are not a good friend. Yet take note that there are no bad friends. By definition of the English dictionary, a friend is a person known well to another and regarded with liking, affection, and loyalty. So you are either a friend or not a friend. If you are rude, mean, insensitive, selfish, a gossiper who spreads confidential information, and are always on the attack, would you befriend somebody who displays this kind of behavior? I think not; and as difficult as this conclusion may be, partially and possibly, it could explain why you do not have any friends! I'm just saying.

In like manner, although you may not have noticed, the best advice you ever gave and give today was to other folk. Isn't that amazing how clearly you see what others need to do to be better, whether they be your friends, children, husbands, wives, choir members, coworkers, etc? You know how to solve their problems. You have much to say when it comes to the solutions for other folk. Yet when you need advice for yourself, you struggle mightily. Other's situations, you know what to do. But yours, you don't seem to have a clue. Why is it that you refuse to accept your advice for yourself? Even when your friend's situations and yours are identical, somehow, you still find a difference and end up making excuses why you should not take the advice you gave to others. You need to be honest with yourself. "Honesty is the best policy."

Find a Friend

David could have avoided much trouble if he had listened to the advice of his friend Joab. The same thing is true for many today. Never think that every idea you have is the best one. The Holy Spirit does influence people, but sometimes, people have influential ideas from the Unholy Spirit! Sometimes, good friends can see what you cannot. It's wise to listen to the counsel of wise Christians, especially for those that think they know everything. At the church I pastor, there's a slogan we use: "Our church is the church where everybody is somebody and nobody but Christ knows it all." Don't make the mistake David made. His pride caused him to follow the provoking of Satan. Pride kept him from listening to God and the wise advice of his friend. Proverbs 16:18 says, "Pride goeth before destruction, and an haughty spirit before a fall."

In 1 Chronicles 21:3, Joab pleaded with David not to be "a cause of trespass (or sin) to Israel" by counting the people. David wanted to see how great his kingdom had become under his leadership. He wanted to know the number of people he had on his side. It appeared that Solomon thought the kingdom was being sustained by the soldiers and the more, the merrier. He thought the presence of the many men was the reason for their many victories against their enemies.

Count the cost

The cost was terrible. David saw the error of his ways later, but it was too late to avoid consequences. God spoke to David through a prophet named Gad. In 1 Chronicles 21:11–12, it says,

> So Gad went to David and said to him, "This is what the Lord says: 'Take your choice: three years of famine, three months of being swept away before your enemies, with their swords overtaking you, or three days of the sword of the Lord—days of plague in the land, with the

angel of the Lord ravaging every part of Israel.' Now then, decide how I should answer the one who sent me."

When Paul and his companions had passed through Amphipolis and Apollonia, they came to Thessalonica, where there was a Jewish synagogue. As was his custom, Paul went into the synagogue, and on three Sabbath days he reasoned with them from the Scriptures, [3] explaining and proving that the Messiah had to suffer and rise from the dead. (Acts 17:1–3)

A trustworthy spiritual partner is needed—someone whose confidentiality and honesty are impeccable, a person whose advice will be considered greatly, and a person who will tell the truth at all times, no matter the consequences.

9

Seeing What You Can't See

So Abraham rose early in the morning and took bread and a skin of water and gave it to Hagar, putting it on her shoulder, along with the child, and sent her away. And she departed and wandered in the wilderness of Beersheba. When the water in the skin was gone, she put the child under one of the bushes. Then she went and sat down opposite him a good way off, about the distance of a bowshot, for she said, "Let me not look on the death of the child. And as she sat opposite him, she lifted up her voice and wept. And God heard the voice of the boy, and the angel of God called to Hagar from heaven and said to her, "What troubles you, Hagar? Fear not, for God has heard the voice of the boy where he is. Lift up the boy, and hold him fast with your hand, for I will make him into a great nation." Then God opened her eyes, and she saw a well of water. And she went and filled the skin with water and gave the boy a drink. (Gen. 21:14–19)

Then the LORD opened the eyes of Balaam, and he saw the angel of the LORD standing in the way, and his sword drawn in his hand: and he bowed down his head, and fell flat on his face. (Num. 22:31)

So he said, "Go and see where he is, that I may send and take him." And it was told him, saying, "Behold, he is in Dothan." He sent horses and chariots and a great army there, and they came by night and surrounded the city. Now when the attendant of the man of God had risen early and gone out, behold, an army with horses and chariots was circling the city. And his servant said to him, "Alas, my master! What shall we do?" So he answered, "Do not fear, for those who are with us are more than those who are with them."

Then Elisha prayed and said, "O LORD, I pray, open his eyes that he may see." And the Lord opened the servant's eyes and he saw; and behold, the mountain was full of horses and chariots of fire all around Elisha. When they came down to him, Elisha prayed to the

Lord and said, "Strike this people with blindness, I pray." So He struck them with blindness according to the word of Elisha. Then Elisha said to them, "This is not the way, nor is this the city; follow me and I will bring you to the man whom you seek." And he brought them to Samaria. When they had come into Samaria, Elisha said, "O Lord, open the eyes of these men, that they may see." So the Lord opened their eyes and they saw; and behold, they were in the midst of Samaria. (2 Kings 6:13–20)

The angel of the Lord encampeth round about them that fear him, and delivereth them. (Ps. 34:7)

For he shall give his angels charge over thee, to keep thee in all thy ways. They shall bear thee up in thy hands. (Ps. 91:11–12)

Now there was a day when the sons of God came to present themselves before the Lord, and Satan came also among them. And the Lord said unto Satan, Whence comest thou? Then Satan answered the Lord, and said, From going to and fro in the earth, and from walking up and down in it. And the Lord said unto Satan, Hast thou considered my servant Job, that there is none like him in the earth, a perfect and an upright man, one that feareth God, and escheweth evil? Then Satan answered the Lord, and said, Doth Job fear God for nought? Hast not thou made an hedge about him, and about his house, and about all that he hath on every side? thou hast blessed the work of his hands, and his substance is increased in the land. But put forth thine hand now, and touch all that he hath, and he will curse thee to thy face. And the Lord said unto Satan, Behold, all that he hath is in thy power; only upon himself put not forth thine hand. So Satan went forth from the presence of the Lord. (Job 1:6–12)

When they heard these things, they were cut to the heart, and they gnashed on him with their teeth. But he, being full of the Holy Ghost, looked up stedfastly into heaven, and saw the glory of God, and Jesus standing on the right hand of God, And said, Behold, I see the heavens opened, and the Son of man standing on the right hand of God. Then they cried out with a loud voice, and stopped their ears, and ran upon him with one accord, And cast him out of the city, and stoned him: and the witnesses laid down their clothes at a young man's feet, whose name was Saul. And they stoned Stephen, calling upon God, and saying, Lord Jesus, receive my spirit. (Acts 7:54–59)

They have mouths, but cannot speak, eyes, but cannot see! (Ps. 135:16)

Do you have eyes but fail to see, and ears but fail to hear. (Mark 8:18)

Hear this now, O foolish people, without understanding, who have eyes and see not, and who have ears and hear not: "Do you not fear me?" says the Lord. "Will you not tremble at my presence, who have placed the sand as the bound of the sea, by a perpetual decree that it cannot pass beyond it? And though its waves toss to and fro, yet they cannot prevail; Though they roar, yet they cannot pass over it." But this people has a defiant and rebellious heart; They have revolted and departed. They do not say in their heart, "Let us now fear the Lord our God, Who gives rain, both the former and the latter, in its season." (Jer. 5:21–24)

They have mouths, but cannot speak, eyes, but cannot see. They have ears, but cannot hear, noses, but cannot smell. They have hands, but cannot feel, feet, but cannot walk, nor can they utter a sound with their throats. (Ps. 115:5–7)

Don't be surprised; just open your eyes.

If you could see what you can't see, you would see that you're gonna see your way through! In other words, if you could see what God sees, you'd see that you're gonna see your way through! You should be more confident in your outlook. Even your walk and talk should be more upbeat. And God knows, if you could see what God sees, you would do more of what God tells you to do! You would not worry about the risks involved. You would be more like Daniel, the three Hebrew boys, Elisha, and even Jesus. If you could see what God sees, you would see that you're gonna see your way through because ultimately, "Those that are with us are more than those that are with them" (2 Kings 6:16).

I hope you can say like I can, "I may not see all I need and want to see, but I sure thank God I see more than I used to see." Hopefully, we can all agree that in our walk with God, we are not where we want and need to be, yet we are nowhere near what we used to be. Yes, we may not see all that is around us and may not see all we need to see physically, spiritually, or emotionally, but at least it's great to be able to say that we see more than we used to see.

I thank God for my newfound vision. I thank God that now I see the need to have God in my life. I have to admit that I haven't always seen the need. Like so many others, back in the day, I did not see the need. I thank

God for allowing me to see the light. Also, I thank God that I now see the need for church in my life. Also I have to admit that I haven't always seen the need. I thank God for my view on family and its importance to living a fulfilled and complete life.

I thank God that I see the need to treat people with kindness and respect; I haven't always seen the need. How about you? Do you see it yet? I thank God that I see the need to edify and build people up rather than tear them down. I see now that tearing people down is the wrong way to build myself up. How about you? Do you see it yet? I thank God for the vision to see what I do see. I can't help but be reminded of the words to "Amazing Grace": "Amazing grace, how sweet the sound. That saved a wretch like me. I once was lost, but now I am found, was blind but now I see."

In Ephesians 4:17–24, Paul says,

> Let me say this, then, speaking for the Lord: Live no longer as the unsaved do, for they are blinded and confused. Their closed hearts are full of darkness; they are far away from the life of God because they have shut their minds against him, and they cannot understand his ways. They don't care anymore about right and wrong and have given themselves over to impure ways. They stop at nothing, being driven by their evil minds and reckless lusts. But that isn't the way Christ taught you! If you have really heard his voice and learned from him the truths concerning himself, then throw off your old evil nature— the old you that was a partner in your evil ways—rotten through and through, full of lust and sham. Now your attitudes and thoughts must all be constantly changing for the better. Yes, you must be a new and different person, holy and good. Clothe yourself with this new nature.

If you could see what you can't see, you would see that you're gonna see your way through! Open your eyes and see what the Lord will do!

The verse 2 Kings 6:14–18 reminds us,

> Therefore sent he thither horses, and chariots, and a great host: and they came by night, and compassed the city about. And when the servant of the man of God was risen early, and gone forth, behold, a host compassed the city both with horses and chariots. And his servant said unto him, Alas, my master! how shall we do? And he

answered, Fear not: for they that be with us are more than they that be with them.

And Elisha prayed, and said, LORD, I pray thee, open his eyes, that he may see. And the LORD opened the eyes of the young man; and he saw: and, behold, the mountain was full of horses and chariots of fire round about Elisha. And when they came down to him, Elisha prayed unto the LORD, and said, Smite this people, I pray thee, with blindness. And he smote them with blindness according to the word of Elisha.

Remember the words of the songwriter:

I never worry I never fret because God almighty has never failed me yet. Rebuke and scorn; you know I been reborn, For God never fails. No need to cry, I'm not afraid to die, I got my Lord, I know He's by my side, Daily I trust Him, Never shall I doubt Him, For God never fails. God never fails, God never fails.

He abides in me, he gives me victory; for God never fails. Just keep the faith and never cease to pray: Walk upright, Call Him day noon or night, He'll be there There's no need to worry, for God never fails.

"They that are with us are more than they that are with them."

Elisha prayed, "Open his eyes, LORD, so that he may see." Then the LORD opened the servant's eyes, and he looked and saw the hills full of horses and chariots of fire all around Elisha. [18] As the enemy came down toward him, Elisha prayed to the LORD, "Strike this army with blindness." So he struck them with blindness, as Elisha had asked.

The text denotes that Syria was north of Israel and made many military thrusts to invade Israel's territory, much like modern Israelis and the Palestinians of our day. Israel's king was able to anticipate these military moves and avoid the battle. Elijah and his young seer, (a prophet in training) were caught up the middle. The king of Aram thought Elisha a problem and the main obstacle standing in his way to victory. So he sent an army to Dothan to capture him. When Elisha's servant saw the vast army surrounding their camp, he panicked. With their backs up against the wall and death seemingly imminent, he turned and cried to Elisha. In turn, Elisha turned to God and asked God to let the young man see what he could not see.

I don't know if you can hear it, but I hear the text singing, "Turn it over to Jesus, turn it over to Jesus, Turn it over to Jesus, he'll make everything all right." When Elisha turned it over to God, God opened his eyes to see what he could not see. He saw horses, chariots and spiritual forces surrounding him and the man of God. If we could see what we cannot see!

There are three points that need making. First, don't be blind to blessings. The servant of Elisha (Gehazi) was so worried about the horsemen and soldiers of Benhadad that it blinded him to the power of Elisha's God. His worrying over his and Elisha's safety over rode his memory of what he had seen God do. He forgot his history with God and had momentary amnesia as to who he was dealing with. Don't ever forget your history with God, and don't forget what God has done for you. Always remember, what God did for you once, he can do it again. Gehazi had seen many of the miracles Elisha performed: (1) the pot of oil of the prophet Obadiah, (2) Elisha blessed the Shunammite woman and her son, (3). Elisha sustains the prophets, and (4) Elisha and Naaman. And just a little while earlier, in fact just minutes removed, Gehazi had witnessed the miracle of the axe head swimming to Elisha.

Yet not long after, the text said, he was afraid. Fear causes man to easily forget God and gravel, gripe and grumble on the ground of ingratitude. Fear makes it easy for man to become negative about life, people and things. To the charge of ingratitude all must plead guilty. Many forget that there are so many possibilities of good, beauty and kindness all around, yet tragically, all that some people see and talk about is the ugliness of the world. Rather than gazing up on the beauty of the stars and moon, many gaze down on the dirt and mud. Rather than looking to the hills from whence cometh our help (as Psalm 121 suggests), many look to the medicine cabinet from when our tranquilizers.

(ILLUS) A RESCUER REJECTED:

Some years ago, an article of *The King's Business* told of a Christian fisherman lying in his boat one night and heard a loud splash not far away. Knowing that the owner of another craft nearby was a heavy drinker, he hurriedly jumped into the cold water and with great effort succeeded in pulling the half-drowned man out of the bay. He carried him to his berth and applied first aid until the alcoholic regained consciousness. Having done everything to make him comfortable, he swam back to his own boat.

The next morning, he returned to inquire how he felt. "That's none of your business," said the man defensively. The fisherman reminded him that he had risked his life to save him; but instead of showing gratitude, the man only cursed him. As the Christian rowed away, tears filled his eyes. Looking up to heaven, he said, "Now I know how you feel when men don't appreciate you.

A couple of weeks ago, I'm sure you heard about the young man who saved a drowning man. The next day, he was fired because he saved the man in the area of the ocean that was outside of his territory of care. Nonappreciation can be a hurtful thing. Let us not be unappreciative.

Lesson number 2: Don't be blind to the pain of people! The king of Israel wanted to smite the enemy, but Elisha said no. We must have concern for people in pain. Consider the hunger all around us, not only those in Kuwait, Jordan, Africa, etc. Look in your town.

A pastor in Kentucky went to school at eight o'clock one morning and found a teacher letting her class eat breakfast. When asked why they were eating breakfast at school and not at home, he was told that 90 percent of the children had no breakfast at home. An empty stomach impairs learning.

There is a song entitled "Look at the Lonely People." There are many people with plenty of money and possessions, but no friends. There are elderly persons who need a note, a call, or a visit from us. Youth too can be lonely with all their activities. They need a friend, a sympathetic listener and someone to believe in them.

An extensive survey was conducted in the United States by a leading polling agency. Questionnaires were distributed to people of various ages and occupations. The key question was this: What are you looking for most in life? When the results were compiled, the analysts were surprised. Most of them had expected answers that would suggest materialistic goals, but the top three things that people wanted in life were love, joy, and peace—the first three fruits of the Spirit!

Lesson number 3: Don't be blind to spiritual resources. When Elisha depended upon God, the Syrians left them never to return. We are like paupers living in an oil-rich land. We live in spiritual poverty because we don't use the keys to our blessings. Prayer and praise.

A couple took a cruise for their honeymoon. They packed peanut butter and crackers to eat because they didn't have any money. They didn't

know that the meals were included and they were invited to eat at the captain's table. Christians can sit at the captain's table. He has paid our debt. Additionally, He cares for us and has the power to supply our need.
Think about Luke 24:36–49, when Jesus appears to the disciples!

> While they were still talking, Jesus himself stood among them and said to them, "Peace be with you. They were startled and frightened, thinking they saw a ghost. He said to them, "Why are you troubled, and why do doubts rise in your minds? Look at my hands and my feet. It is I myself! Touch me and see; a ghost does not have flesh and bones, as you see I have." When he had said this, he showed them his hands and feet. And while they still did not believe it because of joy and amazement, he asked them, "Do you have anything here to eat?" They gave him a piece of broiled fish and he took it and ate it in their presence. He said to them, "This is what I told you while I was still with you: Everything must be fulfilled that is written about me in the Law of Moses, the Prophets and the Psalms." Then he opened their minds so they could understand.

In Psalm 119:12–18, David said,

> Blessed art thou, O LORD: teach me thy statutes. With my lips have I declared all the judgments of thy mouth. I have rejoiced in the way of thy testimonies, as much as in all riches. I will meditate in thy precepts, and have respect unto thy ways. I will delight myself in thy statutes: I will not forget thy word. Deal bountifully with thy servant, that I may live, and keep thy word. Open thou mine eyes, that I may behold wondrous things out of thy law.

Rubbish or reality?

> For the message of the cross is foolishness to those who are perishing, but to us who are being saved it is the power of God. (1 Cor. 1:18)

Just don't be surprised. Open your eyes. Don't be deceived. Just believe.

Open Heart

> And a certain woman named Lydia, a seller of purple, of the city of Thyatira, which worshipped God, heard us: whose heart the Lord

opened, that she attended unto the things which were spoken of Paul. (Acts 16:14)

Open Understanding

"Then opened he their understanding" (Luke 24:45). "And they said one to another, Did not our heart burn within us, while he talked with us by the way, and while he opened to us the scriptures?" (Luke 24:32)

Open up and see the unseeable!

> When the Jews heard these things, they were cut to the heart and they gnashed on him with their teeth. But he, being full of the Holy Ghost, looked up steadfastly into heaven, and saw the glory of God, and Jesus standing on the right hand of God, and said, Behold, I see the heavens opened, and the Son of man standing on the right hand of God. Then they cried out with a loud voice, and stopped their ears, and ran upon him with one accord, And cast him out of the city, and stoned him: and the witnesses laid down their clothes at a young man's feet, whose name was Saul. And they stoned Stephen, calling upon God, and saying, Lord Jesus, receive my spirit. And he kneeled down, and cried with a loud voice, Lord, lay not this sin to their charge. And when he had said this, he fell asleep. (Acts 7:54–60)

1. The greatest service to God that every believer can share is to shine for Him. Not all of us can preach, perform miracles, and contend for the faith like Stephen, but all of us can shine for the Lord as he did—look up Acts 6:15. This is a most gracious ministry that is within the reach of every Christian. Moses experienced the blessing of a shining countenance—look up Exodus 34:29–30 and 35; and of our Lord we read that He was transfigured upon the holy mount—look up Matthew 17:2. We have all met Christians whose faces have literally shone with the glory of the Lord, but what is the secret of a shining countenance? It is an open secret—look up 2 Corinthians 3:18!

2. Spirit-filled workers are always mighty in the Scriptures. Have you noticed this? In Acts 7, Stephen gave a complete survey of Jewish history. What a living illustration he was of 2 Timothy 2:15! Whenever God has a servant whom He is greatly using, you will find that that servant is one who feeds upon and who is filled

with the Word. And to be filled with the Word is the way to be filled with the Holy Spirit, and to be filled with the Holy Spirit is to be filled with the Word.

It is the privilege of every believer to be filled with the Holy Spirit—look up Ephesians 5:18; but the important thing is our *capacity* for the Holy Spirit. A "babe in Christ" may be as truly "filled" as a mature believer; both may be filled, but the capacity of the mature believer is infinitely greater than that of the "babe." The only way to maturity is to feed upon the Word of God, and thus, this is also the way to a greater capacity for His fullness—look up Colossians 3:16.

3. Faithfulness to God and persecution are inseparably linked together. Read Acts 7:54, 58, and 59. Stephen was determined to be faithful to God and to declare all the truth—as we learn from Acts 20:27—and this resulted in his enemies becoming enraged. But Stephen knew that the Lord had said that the pathway of obedience and service would by no means be easy—look up Matthew 5:10–12; John 16:33; Acts 5:41; Philippians 1:29, and 1 Peter 4:12–19, and compare Hebrews 11:34–37. The important thing is to be in God's will and to be submissive to Him, whether it leads to being "sawn in two" or to "escape."

4. True faith endures in trials through seeing Him who is invisible. Of Moses, we read that by faith he did just that—look up Hebrews 11:27; and Stephen did the same—look up Acts 7:54, 58, and 59 and verses 55–56! "When the outlook is bad, try the uplook!" or look up (2 Cor. 12:7–10.) Paul and Silas were able to pray and sing praises to God even when they were suffering in prison. They proved the sufficiency of God's grace to uphold them—look up Acts 16:22–25.

5. A Christian is one who is like Christ. The word means "Christ-like."

> And when he had found him, he brought him unto Antioch. And it came to pass, that a whole year they assembled themselves with the church, and taught much people. And the disciples were called Christians first in Antioch. (Acts 11:26)

6. The blood of the martyrs is the seed of the church. Being a Christian is not only a matter of *profession* (of what we *say*), but of *possession*

(of what we *are*). A Christian is one who possesses Christ, and to possess Him is to become like Him—look up Galatians 2:20 and Colossians 1:27. Stephen was like his Lord; he was meek and lowly, and he prayed for those who despitefully used him—look up Matthew 5:44 and 11:29. In his death, like Jesus, Stephen called upon God—compare Acts 7:59 and Matthew 27:46; he committed his spirit to God—compare Acts 7:59 and Luke 23:46, and see also 1 Peter 4:19; and he prayed for his enemies—compare Acts 7:60 and Luke 23:34. Are we like Jesus?

One of those who watched the stoning of Stephen and listened to his testimony and his dying prayer was Saul of Tarsus—look up Acts 7:58 and 22:20; and there is little doubt that the whole incident wrought deep conviction in the heart and conscience of this young enemy of the gospel. Thus, the death of Stephen was at once fruitful in Saul's conversion (Acts 9:1–17). But that was not the only immediate benefit of his death—look up Acts 11:19. The Christians were scattered, and so the gospel was spread! What a great truth is contained in Philippians 1:12!

7. To the believer, death is but a falling asleep. Note the last three words in Acts 7:60. He had already committed his *spirit* to the Lord (verse 59), but it was his *body* that fell asleep—look up and compare 1 Thessalonians 4:13–17. Stephen was "away from the body" and "at home with the Lord" (2 Cor. 5:6–8). Death = sleep. How beautiful, for sleep means rest after toil, and freedom from fear, sorrow, and all the strain of life. In sleep, we pass from one day to another; and for the Christian, death is the short passage from earth's little day of trouble to heaven's eternal day of glory! You and I may never sleep the sleep of death, but if we do, there need be no fear, for see 1 Corinthians 15:51–58!

When you can see, you not only see yourself, but you see God and what he can do for you.

10

Open Eyes and Closed Minds

> Taste and see that the LORD is good; blessed is the man who takes refuge in Him. (Ps. 34:8)
>
> Open my eyes that I may see wonderful things in your law. (Ps. 119:18)
>
> Then their eyes were opened and they recognized [Jesus]. (Luke 24:31)
>
> For this people's heart has become calloused; they hardly hear with their ears, and they have closed their eyes. Otherwise they might see with their eyes, hear with their ears, understand with their hearts and turn, and I would heal them. (Acts 28:27)

The songwriter said, "Please be patient with me, God is not through with me yet." In order to be blessed on life's journey, there are three characters that must be dealt with: I, Me, and My. Notice Proverbs 29:11: "A fool always loses his temper, but a wise man holds it back."

Also, look up Corinthians 9:26–27: "Therefore I run in such a way, as not without aim; I box in such a way, as not beating the air; but I discipline my body and make it my slave, so that, after I have preached to others, I myself will not be disqualified." To get others to control themselves, you must control yourself.

Mirror, mirror, on the wall, who is fairest of them all? You, you, it's true. The fairest of them all is you, you. Whew, said the wicked queen in the Snow White fairy tale. Romans 12:1–3 says,

> I beseech you therefore, brethren, by the mercies of God, that ye present your bodies a living sacrifice, holy, acceptable unto God, which is your reasonable service. And be not conformed to this world: but be ye transformed by the renewing of your mind that ye may prove; what is that good, acceptable and perfect will of God. For I say, through the

grace given unto me, to every man that is among you, not to think of himself more highly than he ought to think; but to think soberly, according as God hath dealt to every man the measure of faith.

For as we have many members in one body, and all members have not the same office: "so we, being many, are one body in Christ, and every one members one of another. Having then gifts differing according to the grace that is given to us, whether prophecy, let us prophesy according to the proportion of faith; on ministering, let us wait on our ministry, or he that teacheth, on teaching; or he that exhorteth, on exhortation: he that giveth, let him do it with simplicity; he that ruleth, with diligence; he that sheweth mercy, with cheerfulness."

Do not think of yourself more highly than you ought to think!

From Paul's letter to the Romans, we hear these words.

For by the grace given to me I say to everyone among you not to think of yourself more highly than you ought to think, but to think with sober judgment, each according to the measure of faith God has assigned. For as in one body we have many members, and not all the members have the same function, so we, who are many, are one body in Christ, and individually we are members one of another.

These words remind us of the sin of pride and the importance of our relationship one to another.

We all know about pride, but many of us do not associate the sin of pride with God-fearing, card-carrying, faithful-attending members of the church. We often see the sin of pride belonging to someone else. Sometimes the person is described as a "Holy Joe" or someone who has the attitude of being "holier than thou." Yet the sin of pride is often alive and well in our churches. The sin of pride has its root in many forms. Some people believe they are in charge, by some criteria either known or unknown. They believe they have been elevated to the particular position of chief. The criteria may be according to age, tenure, attendance, giving of time or funds, number of responsibilities in the church, or position of the church.

It happens when an individual or individuals begin to think of themselves more highly than they ought. This leads them to step fully into the sin of pride. It is a trap for both the laity and the clergy. For example, when I was a teenager our church did not have a youth group. We had a youth choir. In our youth choir we had four adults to help.

The two adult women started to get on each other's nerves. The issue was over who was in charge. Who was the one to help line everyone up, keep everyone still, and sit in the right places in the choir pews? Their struggle came to a head immediately following the main service one Sunday morning. While on the steps of the church at the end of the procession the two ladies squared off. They were still in their robes. They still had their hymnals in their hands. The confrontation did not end until five men physically separated the two women. About the only thing that can be said is that no punches were thrown.

One final story about pride occurred at a youth meeting. The youth minister was being chastised for visiting all the youth in the parish. Some of the adults on the youth commission were not happy with the visitations. They wanted to know why the youth minister was wasting time visiting children who did not attend church on a regular basis. The youth minister asked one of the parents, "If I only visit those who come, what do you want me to do if your child stops attending regularly?"

The sin of pride exhibited in the church is deadly. It causes unnecessary pain. It creates a hidden hierarchy. It promotes division and destroys community. Pride is the sin that is usually, not always, but usually the center of most church fights. Church fights are horrible. No one wins. Everybody loses. So, what can we do about this sin of pride? How do we address it in ourselves?

Paul gives us a clue. He reminds us that we are all part of one body. As a part of the body we all have gifts. These gifts vary according to each person. Some of the gifts he identifies are prophecy, ministry, teaching, exhortation, giving, leading, and compassion. There is no order to the gifts and these are not the only gifts we could have. Paul's important points are:

1. We all have gifts.
2. The gifts vary from person to person.
3. All these gifts are necessary in the community of the Body of Christ.

We use all of these gifts to God's glory and not to our own. Through the use of our gifts, we deepen our love for God, and we learn how interconnected we are with one another. No one has all the gifts necessary for the community. Have we ever thought to ask the question why did Jesus choose so many disciples? Jesus chose many disciples for the variety of gifts. Community is the key. The moment we begin to believe we can make it on our own we are lost. The moment we begin to believe our gifts are more important than someone else's we are lost. The moment we begin to think we are more important than anyone else in the church we are stepping away from our gifts and into the sin of pride.

Paul gives us an opportunity here. We have an opportunity to examine ourselves and see how we are faring. Are we like the choir members who argued outside the church? Can we see ourselves like the priest before he was hit with the rock? Are we sometimes like the parents who want to determine who gets a visit by attendance at church? If we see ourselves in those veins at times we just might require a little change. In closing I refer again to the poem about the priest who was hit with the stone. The end of the poem is:

> So I guess the moral of this fable is to remember we're all a bit unstable. In church we'd better be more humble and not be too proud or whimsy fall or tumble. Whether ordained or just plain folk, there's nothing wrong with an Easter joke. In fact our young David with his little stone cut the giant Goliath's pride right to the bone.

"Come ye faithful, raise the strain, help us Lord not to be a pain!"

It is from the fairy tale, "Snow White." The evil queen has a magic mirror that she asks on a daily basis, who's the fairest one in the kingdom. Every day the mirror responds you are, until Snow White (her step daughter) begins to grow up. At this time the queen asks, "Mirror, mirror on the wall, who's the fairest of them all" to which the mirror responds "Snow White." Of course the queen then becomes jealous and has a hunter take Snow White to the woods to kill her. The hunter does take her to the woods, but is unable to kill her. He returns to the queen with the heart of a pig to prove that he has killed Snow White. The queen is satisfied. Then asked the mirror again, "Mirror, mirror on the wall, now whose the fairest of them all" the mirror responds "there is one still far more beautiful than thee, Snow White." The queen becomes enraged and then asks the mirror to tell her where she is hidden... The mirror tells her and she begins her plan to kill Snow White, personally.

Now you know the background of the story. The term "mirror, mirror on the wall" is one used to describe vanity and jealousy. The one that sees from the inside out and knows what life is all about, someone who opens up their heart unafraid to let the love come out The mirror on the wall can only see the face you wish it to see. It cannot look deep inside of you, nor see the heart that is soft and true. So when you ask who the fairest might be just look in your heart, and you will see.

The biblical comparison is that before you comment on a "mote" in someone else's eye, one should take the "beam" out of your own. It means that before complaining about little faults in others, we should look to our own big faults.

The reference is made twice in the Gospels, in Matthew and in Luke.

> And why beholdest thou the mote that is in thy brother's eye, but considerest not the beam that is in thine own eye? Or how wilt thou say to thy brother, Let me pull out the mote out of thine eye; and, behold, a beam is in thine own eye? Thou hypocrite, first cast out the beam out of thine own eye; and then shalt thou see clearly to cast out the mote out of thy brother's eye. (Matt. 7:3–5)

Luke 6:41–42 says the same.

"If you could see yourself going wrong, would you stop or go on?"

A new advertising campaign was launched by the Home Office to tackle teen violence. The adverts were directed by the talented Shane Meadows, who was responsible for the critically acclaimed film, *This Is England*. The television, radio, and Internet campaigns tackle both emotional and physical abuse. Even if the campaign saves a handful of girls from abusive relationships, it would have been two million well spent. The Home Secretary Alan Johnson told the BBC:

> *We want to see young people in safe and happy relationships and this means tackling attitudes towards abuse at an early age, before patterns of violence can occur. We hope this campaign will help teenagers to recognize the signs of abuse and equip them with the knowledge and confidence to seek help, as well as understanding the consequences of being abusive or controlling in a relationship.*

This campaign is an essential step towards reducing not only teen violence but also violence towards women in later life. Early detection of physical and emotional abuse quite simply saves lives.

> Do not judge, or you too will be judged. For in the same way you judge others, you will be judged, and with the measure you use, it will be measured to you. Why do you look at the speck of sawdust in your brother's eye and pay no attention to the plank in your own eye? How can you say to your brother, "Let me take the speck out of your eye," when all the time there is a plank in your own eye? You hypocrite, first take the plank out of your own eye, and then you will see clearly to remove the speck from your brother's eye. (Matt. 7:1–5, NIV)

> Then one of them, which was a lawyer, asked him a question, tempting him, and saying, Master, which is the great commandment in the law? Jesus said unto him, Thou shalt love the Lord thy God with all thy heart, and with all thy soul, and with all thy mind. This is the first and great commandment. And the second is like unto it, Thou shalt love thy neighbor as thyself. On these two commandments hang all the law and the prophets. (Matt. 22:35–40)

The text of Matthew 22:35–40 is a clear revelation from the Lord that innately, men and women love themselves. Innately, there is something created within the human family to protect, provide, and preserve their interests. Experience teaches that this built-in prejudice doesn't have to be taught to humans. It automatically or instinctively comes in the box with the birth of every normal human being. Instinctively, babies cry to reveal their discomfort and desire for attention. People without this bias or prejudice (if you will) for self-promotion and self-survival are diagnosed with a variety of dysfunctional ailments. Self-harm, self mutilation, and self-injury are mental health issues treated everyday as an attempt to restore normality to life.

As stated earlier, the most extreme abnormality to self-survival is suicide. The motivation behind the writing of the book was to address this tremendous tragedy among the human family. As the title declares, "If you could see yourself, you wouldn't be yourself!"

Note the story of Dr. Jekyll and Mr. Hyde! The work is commonly associated with the rare mental condition often called "split personality," referred to in psychiatry as *dissociative identity disorder*, where within the same body there exists more than one distinct personality. In this case, there are two personalities within Dr. Jekyll, one apparently good and the other evil. The novella's impact is such that it has become a part of the language, with the very phrase "Jekyll and Hyde" coming to mean a person who is vastly different in moral character from one situation to the next.

Gabriel John Utterson, a lawyer, is on his weekly walk with his cousin, Richard Enfield. During that walk, they reach a door leading into a rather large house, and this motivates Enfield to tell Utterson of an encounter he had seen some months ago while coming home late at night between a man and a young girl. The man, a sinister figure named Edward Hyde, and a young girl, who has run to get a doctor, accidentally bump into one another, but Hyde proceeds to trample her. Enfield chases after Hyde and brings him back to the scene, and after the doctor assures them that the girl is okay, though frightened, he joins with the girl's family in forcing Hyde to pay a hundred dollars to avoid the scandal they will otherwise spread for his despicable behavior.

Hyde leads them to the building in front of which Enfield and Utterson have now paused. He disappears, and reemerges with ten in gold and a check for the rest, drawn on the account of a reputable gentleman. (This gentleman is later revealed to be Dr. Henry Jekyll, one of Utterson's clients and old friends.) Jekyll had recently so draughted his will as to make Hyde the sole beneficiary in case of his death or—much to Utterson's disturbance—his disappearance for more than three months.

This development concerns and disturbs Utterson, who makes an effort to seek out Hyde, fearing that Hyde is blackmailing Jekyll. When he finally sees Hyde, the latter's ugliness, as if deformed, amazes Utterson. Although Utterson cannot say exactly how or why, Hyde provokes an instinctive feeling of revulsion in him. Much to Utterson's surprise, Hyde willingly offers Utterson his address. After one of Jekyll's dinner parties, Utterson stays behind to discuss the matter of Hyde with Jekyll. This causes Jekyll to turn pale, which Utterson notices. Yet Jekyll assures Utterson that everything involving Hyde is in order and that Hyde should be left alone.

To further highlight man's personality problematic positions, there's a related detailing recorded in 2 Samuel 12:1–7:

And the Lord sent Nathan unto David. And he came unto him, and said unto him, there were two men in one city; the one rich, and the other poor. The rich man had exceeding many flocks and herds: but the poor man had nothing, save one little ewe lamb, which he had bought and nourished up: and it grew up together with him, and with his children; it did eat of his own meat, and drank of his own cup, and lay in his bosom, and was unto him as a daughter.

And there came a traveller unto the rich man, and he spared to take of his own flock and of his own herd, to dress for the wayfaring man that was come unto him; but took the poor man's lamb, and dressed it for the man that was come to him. And David's anger was greatly kindled against the man; and he said to Nathan, As the Lord liveth, the man that hath done this thing shall surely die and he shall restore the lamb fourfold, because he did this thing, and because he had no pity. And Nathan said to David, Thou art the man." It was clear, King David could not see himself as others saw him. Even more tragic, he could not see himself as God saw him.

If you could see yourself, you wouldn't be yourself!

What unlimited possibilities and potentials await mankind if and when the goal of this book is reached? The result would be revolutionary, as much so and reforming as the great Reformation of the sixteenth century. Note some of the reforms. According to Wikipedia, the free encyclopedia, The Protestant Reformation was the schism within Western Christianity initiated by Martin Luther, John Calvin, and other early Protestants.

Although there had been significant attempts at reform before Luther (notably those of John Wycliffe and Jan Huss), the date most usually given for the start of the Protestant Reformation is 1517, when Luther published *The Ninety-Five Theses*. Its conclusion in 1648 with the Peace of Westphalia that ended the European wars of religion. Luther started by criticizing the relatively recent practice of selling indulgences, but the debate widened until it touched on many of the doctrines and devotional practices of the Catholic Church.

It led to the creation of New National Protestant Churches. The Reformation changed both church and human history. As reforming, necessary and influential as the Great Reformation was, the need for modern mankind to see themselves as they are seen is more so. The possibilities of greatness for the human race are limitless and catastrophic.

There could literally be "peace on earth." Here's one example to consider. If man could see himself as seen by others, he would not be arrogant, unappreciative and nonchalant about receiving help and assistance from others.

First, the substantiation of the position (when blessed, mankind should be thankful in both word and deed). Luke 17:11–19, Jesus so indicates. Luke records:

> Now on his way to Jerusalem, Jesus traveled along the border between Samaria and Galilee. As he was going into a village, ten men who had leprosy met him. They stood at a distance and called out in a loud voice, "Jesus, Master, have pity on us!" When he saw them, he said, "Go, show yourselves to the priests." And as they went, they were cleansed. One of them, when he saw he was healed, came back, praising God in a loud voice. He threw himself at Jesus' feet and thanked him—and he was a Samaritan. Jesus asked, "Were not all ten cleansed? Where are the other nine? There was no one found to return and give praise to God except this foreigner?" Then he said to him, "Rise and go; your faith has made you well." (NIV)

Please don't miss the Master's great questions in verse 17and 18: "Were not all ten cleansed? Where are the other nine? Was no one found to return and give praise to God except this foreigner?" This is but one example of the Masters teaching on the subject. From it, clearly He prescribes men and women's appreciation for favor from God and man. If the desired result from this one area alone was achieved, the increase, instead of decreased man's desire to go out of his way to for others would be tremendous. Although I recognized the teaching of Jesus on man's assistance to one another should be done automatically by the Christian, such as in Matthew 25:35–40:

> For I was hungry and you gave Me food; I was thirsty and you gave Me drink; I was a stranger and you took Me in; I was naked and you clothed Me; I was sick and you visited Me; I was in prison and you came to Me. Then the righteous will answer Him, saying, "Lord, when did we see you hungry and feed you, or thirsty and give you drink? When did we see you a stranger and take you in, or naked and clothe you? Or when did we see you sick, or in prison, and come to you?"

And the King will answer and say to them, "Assuredly, I say to you, inasmuch as you did it to one of the least of these my brethren, you did it to Me."

But I am still saying to the non-Christian that man's appreciation for assistance would increase man's efforts in this area. Mother used to say, "When somebody does something nice for you, at the very least, show your appreciation and say thank you." Also it needs remembering, as far as the biblical mandates go, that most humans don't read the Bible and many more don't follow God's commands. But if man would correct this one area of concern and just follow the Golden Rule, ("Do unto others as you would have them do unto you," Luke 6:31), it would be revolutionary.

Don't forget both Jesus and his ministry was revolutionary. By definition, revolution is an overthrow or repudiation and the thorough replacement of an established government or political system by the people governed. Jesus changed the course of time (from BC to AD) and human history. The world has not been the same since his arrival. His earthly ministry began at Caesarea Philippi (Matt. 16:13) and continues through the disciples today.

> So Abraham rose early in the morning and took bread and a skin of water and gave it to Hagar, putting it on her shoulder, along with the child, and sent her away. And she departed and wandered in the wilderness of Beersheba. When the water in the skin was gone, she put the child under one of the bushes. Then she went and sat down opposite him a good way off, about the distance of a bowshot, for she said, "Let me not look on the death of the child. And as she sat opposite him, she lifted up her voice and wept. And God heard the voice of the boy, and the angel of God called to Hagar from heaven and said to her, "What troubles you, Hagar? Fear not, for God has heard the voice of the boy where he is. Lift up the boy, and hold him fast with your hand, for I will make him into a great nation." Then God opened her eyes, and she saw a well of water. And she went and filled the skin with water and gave the boy a drink. (Gen. 21:14–19)

> Then the LORD opened the eyes of Balaam, and he saw the angel of the LORD standing in the way, and his sword drawn in his hand: and he bowed down his head, and fell flat on his face. (Num. 22:31)

> So he said, "Go and see where he is, that I may send and take him." And it was told him, saying, "Behold, he is in Dothan." He sent horses

and chariots and a great army there, and they came by night and surrounded the city. Now when the attendant of the man of God had risen early and gone out, behold, an army with horses and chariots was circling the city. And his servant said to him, "Alas, my master! What shall we do?" So he answered, "Do not fear, for those who are with us are more than those who are with them."

Then Elisha prayed and said, "O LORD, I pray, open his eyes that he may see." And the Lord opened the servant's eyes and he saw; and behold, the mountain was full of horses and chariots of fire all around Elisha. When they came down to him, Elisha prayed to the LORD and said, "Strike this people with blindness, I pray." So He struck them with blindness according to the word of Elisha. Then Elisha said to them, "This is not the way, nor is this the city; follow me and I will bring you to the man whom you seek." And he brought them to Samaria. When they had come into Samaria, Elisha said, "O LORD, open the eyes of these men, that they may see." So the LORD opened their eyes and they saw; and behold, they were in the midst of Samaria. (2 Kings 6:13–20)

The angel of the LORD encampeth round about them that fear him, and delivereth them. (Ps. 34:7)

> For he shall give his angels charge over thee, to keep thee in all thy ways. They shall bear thee up in thy hands. (Ps. 91:11–12)

> Now there was a day when the sons of God came to present themselves before the LORD, and Satan came also among them. And the LORD said unto Satan, Whence comest thou? Then Satan answered the LORD, and said, From going to and fro in the earth, and from walking up and down in it. And the LORD said unto Satan, Hast thou considered my servant Job, that there is none like him in the earth, a perfect and an upright man, one that feareth God, and escheweth evil? Then Satan answered the LORD, and said, Doth Job fear God for nought? Hast not thou made an hedge about him, and about his house, and about all that he hath on every side? thou hast blessed the work of his hands, and his substance is increased in the land. But put forth thine hand now, and touch all that he hath, and he will curse thee to thy face. And the LORD said unto Satan, Behold, all that he hath is in thy power; only upon himself put not forth thine hand. So Satan went forth from the presence of the LORD. (Job 1:6–12)

> When they heard these things, they were cut to the heart, and they gnashed on him with their teeth. But he, being full of the Holy Ghost, looked up stedfastly into heaven, and saw the glory of God, and Jesus standing on the right hand of God, And said, Behold, I see the heavens opened, and the Son of man standing on the right hand of God. Then they cried out with a loud voice, and stopped their ears, and ran upon him with one accord, And cast him out of the city, and stoned him: and the witnesses laid down their clothes at a young man's feet, whose name was Saul. And they stoned Stephen, calling upon God, and saying, Lord Jesus, receive my spirit. (Acts 7:54–59)

The fact that humans can't see themselves as others see them has brought about complete chaos and devastation.

One again reiterating, it helps to acknowledge song, "Please be patient with me, God is not through with me yet." In order to be blessed on life's journey, there are three people that must be controlled; me, myself and I. It is a reminder set at the entrance of the book to highlight the Church's creation and mission. When humans can't see themselves as they are seen by others chaos and devastation follows. But don't get discouraged IF YOU COULD SEE, WHAT YOU CAN'T SEE, you would see that you're gonna see your way through!

Because if you could see what God sees, you would see that you're gonna see your way through! You would be more confident in your outlook. Even your walk and talk would be more upbeat. And God knows, If you could see what God sees, you would do more of what God tells you to do! You would not worry about the risks involved. You would be more like Daniel or the 3 Hebrew boys. If you could see what God sees, you would see that you're gonna see your way through because ultimately, "Those that are with us are more than those that are with them."

Foundation Scriptures

> The Lord sent Nathan to David. When he came to him, he said, "There were two men in a certain town, one rich and the other poor. The rich man had a very large number of sheep and cattle, but the poor man had nothing except one little ewe lamb he had bought. He raised it, and it grew up with him and his children. It shared his food, drank from his cup and even slept in his arms. It was like a daughter to him.

"Now a traveler came to the rich man, but the rich man refrained from taking one of his own sheep or cattle to prepare a meal for the traveler who had come to him. Instead, he took the ewe lamb that belonged to the poor man and prepared it for the one who had come to him. David burned with anger against the man and said to Nathan, 'As surely as the Lord lives, the man who did this must die! He must pay for that lamb four times over, because he did such a thing and had no pity.'

Then Nathan said to David, 'You are the man! This is what the Lord, the God of Israel, says: "I anointed you king over Israel, and I delivered you from the hand of Saul. I gave your master's house to you, and your master's wives into your arms. I gave you all Israel and Judah. And if all this had been too little, I would have given you even more. Why did you despise the word of the Lord by doing what is evil in his eyes? You struck down Uriah the Hittite with the sword and took his wife to be your own. You killed him with the sword of the Ammonites. Now, therefore, the sword will never depart from your house, because you despised me and took the wife of Uriah the Hittite to be your own"… Then David said to Nathan, 'I have sinned against the Lord.'" (2 Sam. 12:1–10, 13)

Woe to those who are wise in their own eyes, and shrewd in their own sight! (Isa. 5:21, ESV)

Do not judge, or you too will be judged. For in the same way you judge others, you will be judged, and with the measure you use, it will be measured to you. Why do you look at the speck of sawdust in your brother's eye and pay no attention to the plank in your own eye? How can you say to your brother, "Let me take the speck out of your eye," when all the time there is a plank in your own eye? You hypocrite, first take the plank out of your own eye, and then you will see clearly to remove the speck from your brother's eye. (Matt. 7:1–5, NIV)

Then one of them, which was a lawyer, asked him a question, tempting him, and saying, "Master, which is the great commandment in the law?" Jesus said unto him, Thou shalt love the Lord thy God with all thy heart, and with all thy soul, and with all thy mind. [38] This is the first and great commandment. And the second is like unto it, Thou shalt love thy neighbor as thyself. On these two commandments hang all the law and the prophets. (Matt. 22:35–40)

And when he came to himself. (Luke 15:17)

11

You Can Catch More Flies with Honey

Overcoming negative attributes

You have heard that it was said, "Eye for eye, and tooth for tooth." But I tell you, do not resist an evil person. If anyone slaps you on the right cheek, turn to them the other cheek also. And if anyone wants to sue you and take your shirt, hand over your coat as well. If anyone forces you to go one mile, go with them two miles. Give to the one who asks you, and do not turn away from the one who wants to borrow from you. (Matt. 5:38–42)

Then said Jesus unto his disciples, "If any man will come after me, let him deny himself, and take up his cross, and follow me." (Matt. 16:24)

Do nothing from selfishness or empty conceit, but with humility of mind regard one another as more important than yourselves; do not merely look out for your own personal interests, but also for the interests of others. Have this attitude in yourselves which was also in Christ Jesus, who, although He existed in the form of God, did not regard equality with God a thing to be grasped, but emptied Himself, taking the form of a bond-servant, and being made in the likeness of men. Being found in appearance as a man, He humbled Himself by becoming obedient to the point of death, even death on a cross. For this reason also, God highly exalted Him, and bestowed on Him the name which is above every name, so that at the name of Jesus every knee will bow, of those who are in heaven and on earth and under the earth, and that every tongue will confess that Jesus Christ is Lord, to the glory of God the Father. (Phil. 2:3–11)

The old saying is, "You can catch more flies with honey than vinegar." Think about this: it is easier to get what you want with flattery and politeness than by making demands and rudeness.

> Jill: This meal is terrible. Let's get the restaurant manager over here and make a scene unless he gives us our money back.
>
> Jane: We might have more success if we ask politely. You can catch more flies with honey than with vinegar.

Look at it this way: don't be selfish with time, energy, attention, and money. If you are bitterly jealous and there is selfish ambition in your heart, don't cover up the truth, lying, or boasting with pride. For jealousy and selfishness are not God's kind of wisdom. Such things are earthly, unspiritual, and demonic. James said, "For wherever there is jealousy and selfish ambition, there you will find disorder and evil of every kind" (James 3:14–16 (NLT). Selfishness can change your heavenly happiness into a living hell for you and everybody around you.

Overcoming selfishness is a move towards abundant living. Jesus said, "I am come that you might life and have it more abundantly" (John 10:10b). Selfishness is a roadblock to a happier more peaceful life. Overcoming selfishness takes work…some things will not be easy!

How to Overcome Selfishness

1. Admit your selfishness and be honest about it. The first step in overcoming selfishness is to first admit it to yourself. This can often be one of the hardest steps. It isn't easy for us to look ourselves in the mirror and honestly recognize we are selfish. Maybe it is self-preservation? Admittedly, admitting ugly things about ourselves hurts, and all people want to avoid pain.

    On the other hand, which is worse, admitting being selfish or continuing to live selfish lives and suffering the consequences? Admitting the truth about ourselves can be a great relief. It will free you to let go and begin healing. There is no other way to begin the process.

2. Begin to give generously when you least want to (time, energy, attention, and money). Learn to invest into something else other than yourself. Luke 6:38 says, "Give and it shall be given unto

you." Don't worry about people taking advantage over you. Let the Lord deal with them.

When you feel the most resistance to giving in, just do it! When your family, friends, church, etc. need your time, energy, attention, and money. Give it! As you do this, it will slowly become easier. It's very important to make this right decision in the crucial moments of choice. A circumstance will soon arise where you feel a strong pull to insist on getting your way. Don't fall to it! Instead, see it as an opportunity to conquer self. God will present opportunities to you for you to exercise unselfishness. Take advantage of those opportunities.

3. Be patient with those who have endured your selfishness! Even though you have admitted your selfishness to yourself and started to fight against it, don't expect everyone else to jump on the bandwagon too soon. They've been hurt, victimized, and suffered by you. The people around you endured your selfishness far too long; to immediately believe it is now over. In their eyes, you may relapse at any time.

Sometimes, they may want to see a long track record of generosity, kindness, and thoughtfulness before they are going to fully accept the new you. Be patient with them. Give them time to see that you are serious and committed to overcoming your selfishness.

At the end of your day, examine yourself to see if you were selfish towards your family, coworkers, or even those you came into contact with through the course of your day. (Examine your thoughts, words, attitude, and actions.)

Judge yourself! The Scripture says,

> Judge not, that you be not judged. For with what judgment you judge, you will be judged; and with the measure you use, it will be measured back to you. And why do you look at the speck in your brother's eye, but do not consider the plank in your own eye? Or how can you say to your brother, 'Let me remove the speck from your eye'; and look, a plank *is* in your own eye? Hypocrite! First remove the plank from your own eye, and then you will see clearly to remove the speck from your brother's eye. (Matt. 7:1–5)

In other words, if you judge yourself properly, you will not judge others. You will see your own faults. Therefore, be honest with yourself and stay away from blaming others and making excuses. Repent of those things you believe the Lord is revealing to you. You will have another opportunity to make it right. Make it a point to do something for somebody other than yourself; become a servant.

4. Walk in love. Make 1 Corinthians 13:1–8 a daily meditation until it becomes big in you. John 13:34–35 says, "Little children, I am with you a little while longer. You will seek Me; and as I said to the Jews, now I also say to you, 'Where I am going, you cannot come.' A new commandment I give to you, that you love one another, even as I have loved you, that you also love one another. "By this all men will know that you are My disciples, if you have love for one another." The greatest thing you can do to your fellow man is to walk in love towards them. Love kills selfishness. You have to start killing the fleshly monster inside of you that constantly annoys and tempts you to get its way.

Overcome meanness

A soft answer turns away wrath, but a harsh word stirs up anger. (Prov. 15:1)

Be kind to one another, tenderhearted, forgiving one another, as God in Christ forgave you. (Eph. 4:32)

Bearing with one another and, if one has a complaint against another, forgiving each other; as the Lord has forgiven you, so you also must forgive. (Col. 3:13)

For such men are false apostles, deceitful workmen, disguising themselves as apostles of Christ. And no wonder, for even Satan disguises himself as an angel of light. So it is no surprise if his servants, also, disguise themselves as servants of righteousness. Their end will correspond to their deeds. (1 Cor. 11:13–15)

So put away all malice and all deceit and hypocrisy and envy and all slander. Like newborn infants, long for the pure spiritual milk, that by it you may grow up into salvation—if indeed you have tasted that the Lord is good. As you come to him, a living stone rejected by men but in the sight of God chosen and precious, you yourselves like living stones are being built up as a spiritual house, to be a holy priesthood, to offer spiritual sacrifices acceptable to God through Jesus Christ. (1 Pet. 2:1–5)

Mean-spirited slander is heartless; quiet discretion accompanies good sense. A gadabout gossip can't be trusted with a secret, but someone of integrity won't violate a confidence. Without good direction, people lose their way; the more wise counsel you follow, the better your chances. Whoever makes deals with strangers is sure to get burned; if you keep a cool head, you'll avoid rash bargains. A woman of gentle grace gets respect, but men of rough violence grab for loot. When you're kind to others, you help yourself; when you're cruel to others, you hurt yourself. Bad work gets paid with a bad check; good work gets solid pay. Take your stand with God's loyal community and live, or chase after phantoms of evil and die. God can't stand deceivers, but oh how he relishes integrity. Count on this: The wicked won't get off scot-free, and God's loyal people will triumph. Like a gold ring in a pig's snout is a beautiful face on an empty head. (Prov. 11:12–22)

Overcome hatred in your heart

If anyone says, "I love God," and hates his brother, he is a liar; for he who does not love his brother whom he has seen cannot love God whom he has not seen. (1 John 4:20)

Hatred stirs up strife, but love covers all offenses. (Prov. 10:12)

Everyone who hates his brother is a murderer, and you know that no murderer has eternal life abiding in him. (1 John 3:15)

There are six things that the Lord hates, seven that are an abomination to him: haughty eyes, a lying tongue, and hands that shed innocent blood, a heart that devises wicked plans, feet that make haste to run to evil, a false witness who breathes out lies, and one who sows discord among brothers. (Prov. 6:16–19)

You shall not hate your brother in your heart, but you shall reason frankly with your neighbor, lest you incur sin because of him. (Lev. 19:17)

Let no corrupting talk come out of your mouths, but only such as is good for building up, as fits the occasion, that it may give grace to those who hear. (Eph. 4:29)

Love is patient and kind; love does not envy or boast; it is not arrogant or rude. It does not insist on its own way; it is not irritable or resentful; it does not rejoice at wrongdoing, but rejoices with the truth. Love bears all things, believes all things, hopes all things, endures all things. (1 Cor. 13:4–7)

For this reason God gave them up to dishonorable passions. For their women exchanged natural relations for those that are contrary to nature; and the men likewise gave up natural relations with women and were consumed with passion for one another, men committing shameless acts with men and receiving in themselves the due penalty for their error. (Rom. 1:26–27)

A soft answer turns away wrath, but a harsh word stirs up anger. (Prov. 15:1)

A new commandment I give to you, that you love one another: just as I have loved you, you also are to love one another. By this all people will know that you are my disciples, if you have love for one another. (John 13:34–35)

The fear of the Lord is hatred of evil. Pride and arrogance and the way of evil and perverted speech I hate. (Prov. 8:13)\

Whosoever says he is in the light and hates his brother is still in darkness. (1 John 2:9)

Overcoming Arrogance

Meekness and Humility: God's Cure for Pride, Haughtiness, and Egotism.

Why should people be meek and humble? What problems are caused by pride, arrogance, ego, self-exaltation, haughtiness, and self-will? Should you learn self-assertiveness, or should you learn not to be proud and haughty? What does the Bible teach about meekness, humility, gentleness, and lowliness in contrast to pride, selfishness, self-will, and arrogance?

Moses and Jesus possessed the qualities we want to study in this lesson.

Moses was very meek, above all men on face of the earth. (Num. 12:3)

Jesus said, "I am meek and lowly in heart. (Matt. 11:29:30)

These men were two of the greatest characters who ever lived. Both were chosen by God to be givers of His law. Jesus was the Divine Son of God. Surely we should seek to be like these men.

Here are a few other verses that emphasize the importance of these qualities!

> Blessed are the meek [gentle, NKJV], for they shall inherit the earth. (Matt. 5:5)

Jesus declares a "blessing" (happiness) on those who are meek.

> Meekness is one of the fruits of the Spirit—qualities that we must possess if we are led by the Spirit. (Gal. 5:22–23)
>
> Pride goes before destruction and a haughty spirit before a fall. It is better to be of a humble spirit with the lowly. If we seek happiness, the leading of the Spirit, avoidance of destruction, and to be like great people such as Moses and Jesus, we need to possess meekness and humility. (Prov. 16:18–19)

It is the purpose of this chapter to study these qualities, what they are, and how they will affect our lives. As we study, we will frequently note Moses and Jesus as examples who teach us about meekness and humility.

"Meekness" is an extremely difficult word to translate into English because we think "meek" implies weakness. Sometimes it is translated (NKJV) "gentleness," but that also implies weakness.

The best way to know the meaning of a word is to study passages where it is used. As we do, we will see meekness is an attitude or quality of heart (1 Pet. 3:4) whereby a person willingly accepts and submits without resistance to the will and desires of someone else. The meek person is not self-willed—not continually concerned with self, his own ways, ideas, and wishes. He is willing to put himself in second place and submit himself to achieve what is good for others. Meekness is the opposite of self-will, self-interest, and self-assertiveness. This is a sign, not of weakness of character (as some think), but of strength. It requires great self-control to submit to others.

Humility is an attitude or quality of mind (Acts 20:19) whereby a person holds low esteem or opinion of his own goodness and importance. Spiritually, one abases himself because he realizes his sinfulness and therefore he is willing to depend on God to meet His needs. It is the opposite of pride, haughtiness, and self-exaltation.

Meekness and humility toward God: In the Bible, meekness is primarily emphasized as submissiveness toward God rather than toward men. As directed toward God, meekness and humility require the following:

We must recognize our sinfulness and our dependence on God. We must recognize our sinfulness.

Luke 18:9–14

A Pharisee trusted in himself that he was righteous, prayed with himself, thanking God he was better than other people. Note the Pharisee's emphasis on self, exaltation of self, and his failure to see his sins. The publican pleaded for mercy admitting he was a sinner. Note the conclusion in verse 14: One who exalts self will be abased, one who humbles self will be exalted! Humility is the opposite of self-exaltation and self-righteousness.

A preacher once preached a sermon on this story and afterward a man prayed, "Lord, we thank thee that we are not proud like that Pharisee!" He was doing the very thing he was saying he was not doing! We are all sinners. We have no right to look down on anyone as if we deserve salvation because we are so good, and they don't deserve it. We can be more righteous than the Pharisee, but only by humbling ourselves like the publican and calling on God to forgive us.

1 John 1:8, 10 says, "If we say we have not sinned, we are liars." We are all sinners, and often need forgiveness. We all deserve to be punished for our sins. We have hope of salvation only by God's gracious willingness to forgive. We are no better than the Pharisee or publican, in the sense we are all sinners.

B. Depend on God. Note the example of Moses in Deuteronomy 8:3, 11–14,16–18. Moses knew that man lives, not by bread alone, but by the word of God. Our physical blessings come, not by our own power and might, but from God. All good things come from God.

Appreciate how weak we would be without Him. This leads us to depend on God to meet our needs. In turn, we then appreciate and exalt Him. Note the teaching of Jesus in Matthew 18:1–4. The greatest in the kingdom is one who is humble like a little child. I have heard people say a child is humble because it is forgiving. Perhaps, but a child is not just forgiving; he is totally dependent on his parents. Where does a child receive what he needs? Who provides his food, changes his diaper, and dresses him? When he has pain, for whom does he call? A child is weak, but he knows Momma and Daddy can meet his needs. So humility leads us to humbly admit our need for God.

Proper humility toward God is an admission of our own weakness, sinfulness, unprofitability and inability to obtain or accomplish by ourselves the things we need. We need help from someone far greater than we are. God knows what we need and what is good better than we know, and He has power to do what needs done. Humility will lead us to appreciate Him, trust His will, and give Him the glory, rather than exalting self.

II. We must submit to God's commands. If we know our weaknesses and our tendency to err, in contrast to God's wisdom and power, we should be willing to do what He says. We should believe that His will is best and that we will receive His aid only if we obey Him.

Note the examples of Moses and of Jesus! A. The example of Moses! Numbers 12:3, 6, 7. He was very meek. He was faithful in all God's house. Exodus 40:16: He did according to all that Jehovah commanded him, so did he. Hebrews 8: He built all things according to the pattern shown him.

B. The example of Jesus! "Having come to earth as a man, Jesus humbled Himself and became obedient, even to the point of dying on the cross" (Phil. 2:8). Hebrews 4:15 and 1 Cor. 10:13: He was tempted in all points like we are yet without sin. 1 Peter 2:21, 22: He left us an example that we should follow His steps. He did no sin nor was guilt found in His mouth.

Both Moses and Jesus are expressly noted for their meekness and humility, and both were thoroughly obedient to God. B. Applications to Us! James 1:21–25: Meekness toward God's word requires putting away filth and wickedness. Be doers of the word, not just hearers. James 4:6–10: God resists the proud, but gives grace to the humble. Humble yourselves in the sight of God and He will exalt you. Therefore be subject to God, draw nigh to Him, cleanse your hands, purify your hearts, be afflicted, mourn, and weep. This is the true effect of humility in our lives, just as in Jesus's life (cf. 1 Peter 1:22).

When we are truly humble, and hold ourselves in low esteem compared to God's exalted greatness, we will submit to His will. This is why Scripture so often associates repentance with humbling oneself (1 Kings 21:27; 2 Chron. 7:13; Isa. 57:15; 1 Pet. 5:5–9; Prov. 15:31–33).

Matthew 16:24: Here is an excellent definition of "meekness," without using the word. To be meek is to deny self. The selfish person says "I want this, I want that." True meekness says, "So what! What does God want?" Is this really best according to God's way? God's ways are so much better than ours that we will submit.

Someone says, "Well, don't we ever get to consider what we want?" Yes, but be careful. When it doesn't matter according to God's will, then we may consider our own will. But the meek person carefully considers God's will first, then his own will last. It is very easy to sub-consciously desire to please ourselves, so we conclude an act doesn't matter to God, when really it does matter to Him. We must question every act, word, thought as to what effect it will have on our service to God. Then we do only what we are sure will please God.

III. We must accept circumstances of life according to God's will.

A meek and humble person will accept persecution, mistreatment, suffering, or hardship without rebelling against God and without doubting His wisdom. We will accept the fact that He has chosen to allow this to happen for His good purposes.

A. Learn from the following examples of Moses and Jesus! Example of Moses: Numbers 11:10–15: Moses had problems most of us would never submit to. People constantly complained about his leadership, even though he was just doing what God said. How many of us would have stood for it? No wonder he was called the meekest man on earth! In fact, it was a complaint against him that occasioned the statement that he was so meek (12:1–3).

Example of Jesus: Acts 8:32–33–He was led as a sheep to the slaughter (Isa. 53:7f). Matthew 26:39: Was it hard for Jesus to go to the "slaughter?" Did this take meekness? He said, "Not my will but thine be done." Philippians 2:8: Jesus left the glory of heaven, humbled Himself and became obedient to the point of the death on the cross. Consider how much humility and meekness would be required for one to willingly leave the glory of heaven to come to earth to live as a man and die as a criminal to save others.

B. Applying the principles. Notice Hebrews 12:2–6,

> Looking unto Jesus the author and finisher of our faith; who for the joy that was set before him endured the cross, despising the shame,

and is set down at the right hand of the throne of God. For consider him that endured such contradiction of sinners against himself, lest ye be wearied and faint in your minds. Ye have not yet resisted unto blood, striving against sin. And ye have forgotten the exhortation which speaketh unto you as unto children, My son, despise not thou the chastening of the Lord, nor faint when thou art rebuked of him:[6] For whom the Lord loveth he chasteneth, and scourgeth every son whom he receiveth. (Heb. 12:2–6)

Jesus was and is our example. We should be willing to submit to suffering just as He did. We have suffered nothing like He, yet we often rebel against self-sacrifice. Deuteronomy 8:1–5, 15, 16, notes:

> All the commandments which I command thee this day shall ye observe to do, that ye may live, and multiply, and go in and possess the land which the LORD sware unto your fathers. And thou shalt remember all the way which the LORD thy God led thee these forty years in the wilderness, to humble thee, and to prove thee, to know what was in thine heart, whether thou wouldest keep his commandments, or no. And he humbled thee, and suffered thee to hunger, and fed thee with manna, which thou knewest not, neither did thy fathers know; that he might make thee know that man doth not live by bread only, but by every word that proceedeth out of the mouth of the LORD doth man live. Thy raiment waxed not old upon thee, neither did thy foot swell, these forty years. Thou shalt also consider in thine heart, that, as a man chasteneth his son, so the LORD thy God chasteneth thee.

God allows circumstances that chasten us in order to keep us humble, submissive to His will, and dependent on Him. The difficult circumstances always end up to our advantage.

Most of the time people want to control their own lives. People get panicky when they feel unable to do anything about problems they don't want to face. But facing hardships that we cannot solve alone helps make us humble. The message is that when we see our weaknesses, we turn to God for help. It's good to appreciate Him and acknowledge our need for Him.

This does not mean we should blame God for causing all problems that come, nor does it mean we only have problems when we sin. Sometimes our problems are caused by our own sins. But other times, like Job, we have not sinned, but God allows Satan to cause hardships to test our loyalties. As James 1:13–14 says, "Let no man say when he is tempted, I am tempted of God: for God cannot be tempted with evil, neither tempteth he any man: But every man is tempted, when he is drawn away of his own lust, and enticed." Satan is ultimately responsible for the existence of troubles, but God uses them to make us humble.

Note 2 Corinthians 12:7–10: Paul's thorn in the flesh kept him from being overly exalted. Satan, not God, brought the problem. But God allowed it to remain, because it produced humility and goodness for Paul. So problems can be a blessing because they keep us from becoming proud and self-reliant. This does not mean we should put ourselves in hard circumstances, nor avoid improving our circumstances. If we can escape our problems, we should do so and give thanks to God. But if He chooses to allow the problem to continue, we should not blame Him but appreciate the lessons such problems can teach us. Hardships work for our good if we endure faithfully. The meek and humble person realizes this and submits without rebelling or being bitter against God.

"Thanks be to God for all of his blessings to the children of men."

I hope and pray that this book has been a blessing. If it has, don't keep the information to yourself, recommend it to another and bless them.